God's
"Bad Boys"

GOD'S
"BAD BOYS"

Charles Emerson Boddie

Judson Press
Valley Forge

GOD'S "BAD BOYS"

Copyright © 1972
Judson Press
Valley Forge, Pa. 19481

Except where otherwise noted, the Bible quotations in this volume are in
accordance with the King James Version.

Other versions which have been quoted as indicated in the text are: the
Revised Standard Version of the Bible, copyright 1946 and 1952 by the
Division of Christian Education of the National Council of the Churches
of Christ in the United States of America, used by permission, and
The Bible: A New Translation by James Moffatt. Copyright 1954 by James
Moffatt. Reprinted by permission of Harper & Row, Publishers, Inc.

Library of Congress Cataloging in Publication Data

Boddie, Charles Emerson.

God's bad boys.

1. Negro clergy—United States—Biography.

I. Title.
BR563.N4B64   253'.2'0922[B]   72-75360
ISBN 0-8170-0534-X

Printed in the U.S.A.

To
Mabel

Foreword

In pulling together these engaging accounts of God's "Bad Boys,"
Charles Emerson Boddie renders a service of immeasurable
value. The result of this painstaking research and personal obser-
vation is an exciting collection of biographical sketches of eight
gifted and resourceful leaders in the Christian church. But this
is no ordinary "Who's Who Among the Christian Clergy." This
is an assemblage of God's ebony prophets whose stories, for the
most part, would never be told on the printed page — except for
the insights and efforts of such writers as Dr. Boddie.

The fact that those who record American church history
would hardly mention many of these persons in their accounts
does not in any way mean that these men are less than those
whose stories are included in the rank and file records. The fact
that the subjects of *God's "Bad Boys"* are black has brought
about their exclusion from the accepted list of leaders in the
American church. These men are leaders in an entire corpus of
experience which is a part of what is called the black experience,
although this experience is considered to be a little more than
an amusing aside by those who deign to tell the stories of American church fathers.

We must confess, however, that there are now a few persons who are making a genuine effort to take the remedial steps and to fill in the spaces left vacant by racist selectivity. These efforts will be greatly helped by God's "Bad Boys."

Those whose stories are told here are black leaders. This means that they are not confined to that institution called the church — in this case, the black church. It means that they are leaders in the black community and in the larger community. The black community and the black religious community are virtually indistinguishable. By and large, a black religious leader is simply a black leader or, in an even truer sense, simply a leader. The black pastor who is truly a leader cannot remain in his pulpit without becoming involved in many activities and issues beyond the four walls of his church. His members are also victims of oppression. His church building is often located in a neighborhood which dramatizes the worst disease of American society. His church is one of the few agencies of the black community where there are regular meetings, and it is the only mass agency which the black community owns. Whether the black religious leader's involvement in the crucial issues of the community is considered part or parcel of his formal ministry or whether it is, as some have suggested, "non-theological" (is there any such thing?), it must be confessed that it is an urgent leadership without which our society would be greatly impoverished.

Most of those included in God's "Bad Boys" possessed charisma. Although charisma is not the underlying reason for their inclusion in this book, it is a characteristic that is helpful and meaningful as one seeks to fulfill his ministry in the total community.

These men used traditional methods as they faced new situations and circumstances. Many times they applied unused or untried methods which were culturally approved, and thereby they were creative and innovative. They were truly great leaders.

Each man here possessed that irreplaceable quality of black leaders, especially black preachers: the ability to "tell the story"! Each in his own way was a master of the art of communicating with the masses, particularly the black masses. Not a few of them could communicate with the masses and the classes with ease and effectiveness. The expression "bad boys" as used in the title of this book is well known in the black religious community. When a man can "tell the story" with profundity and poetical beauty, with hope which does not skim over grave problems, with the sense of celebration which so characterizes the black church — in short with thorough mastery of the art of preaching — the black religious community bestows upon him the high compliment of being called a "bad boy."

KELLY MILLER SMITH

The Divinity School
Vanderbilt University
August, 1972

Preface

Preaching as a profession has fallen upon evil times. If there is any likelihood of its once again becoming a preferred calling, it will be with the help of life sketches like these directed toward a generation that "knows not Joseph," with the hope that an urge to discover a lost radiance may be provoked. These sketches are meant to capture the imagination of today's reader who has been caught in the contemporaneity of the "swinger" who thinks of all things *mod* as *mad*, all things *good* as *bad*. Here are some little biographies of black preachers, most of whom are of recent vintage, who represent a style of life and leadership that seldom has been noticed. Not all are "God's Trombones," but all are God-enthralled servants of the black church in America, whose right to be is not apologized for in terms of deft but deadly stereotype. Black and beautiful are they in proud ways. They are scholars, endowed with intellectual and forensic gifts supporting those of like skill and intent in the common struggle to dynamite the darkness of ignorance that bedevils mankind.

Finished is their earthly work, but unended is the importance which yet clings to their attainments and the tremendous influence which they still exert. That they are Baptists is incidental. That they are God's "Bad Boys" compels this attempt to enshrine them in eternal memory. For the inspiring assistance of my wife, Mabel Bell Crooks Boddie; and for that of a son, C. Harreld Rose, and surviving wives of some of the "bad boys," Altona Johns, Pearl McNeil, Emery Boddie, and Lillian Barbour; that of my secretary, Lucile M. Campbell; and that of Frank T. Hoadley, David T. Shannon, Ellwood Wolf, and Harold Twiss, along with those whose friendly persuasion encouraged them to move out with some risk to publish these accounts, no statement here can exhaust my gratitude.

CHARLES EMERSON BODDIE

American Baptist Theological Seminary
August, 1972

Contents

Contents

God's
"Bad Boys"

Russell Conwell Barbour

"Hello, Russell Conwell Barbour. Welcome home."

"Hello, Russell Herman Conwell. It's good to be here." Thus two men greeted each other, recognizing the similarity of their names. The greeting was amazing identification, as well as amazing grace!

The accomplishments of these two men ran nearly parallel. Russell H. Conwell was a pastor, an educator, and a lecturer. Russell Conwell Barbour was a pastor, an educator, and an editor. Certainly it must be said that the latter erected a great temple in the form of his inspiring influence that was pumped into the lives of students who sat at his feet and who still continue to sing his praises.

The pastor-founder of Temple University not only won fame by delivering his famous lecture "Acres of Diamonds" more than six thousand times, but he also won a loyal disciple in the person of Alfred Barbour. This disciple was so impressed that at the birth of his son on December 8, 1897, in Galveston, Texas, he bestowed upon him the names Russell Conwell to precede his surname. When this son grew up, it was found that his vocational talents, so like those of the man for whom he was named, brought fame to him as he walked among his peers, serving his fellow black brothers.

Somewhere it is recorded that good food, good parents, and good books produce good persons. Russell Conwell Barbour, parsonage born, grew into the full maturity which is watered by the springs from which flow such physical, moral, and spiritual sustenance. He was baptized by his father when he was ten years old. Russell's mother, Ellen, bore the maiden name "MacBeth," but none of the bizarre mentality of the Lady Macbeth of the bard was to be discovered in the Barbour bloodline.

Russell had two brothers and two sisters. The elder brother, now the Reverend J. Pius Barbour, a well-known cleric in Chester, Pennsylvania, carries reminders of the papal establishment, one by his name and the other by his mien and generous girth, resembling the figure of the great John XXIII. For more than forty years, this brother has been serving with distinction —the Sage of Chester — as one of the area's most influential religious leaders. The younger brother, John Henry, an attorney, did not attain the notoriety of the renowned Chester veteran. Of the two sisters, the younger, Lidge, passed away in infancy, but the elder, Sally, was a great favorite of Russell and of the family's neighborhood.

INTO NO HAVEN

Too early, it seemed, interrupting his college education at Colgate, his father's pastoral mantle fell upon his shoulders, making firm a ministerial dynasty in the Galveston church. This unexpected circumstance contained ingredients which might have brought about disaster. Russell not only inherited the grave responsibility of carrying the ball for "Pop," but he also assumed this burden without a helpmate. The eight intervening years between his installation as pastor and his marriage must have been fraught with pitfalls and snares which only the adroitness and rare intelligence of one so richly endowed could have so successfully sidestepped. How true this must have been when, later, his widow could say, "Everybody loved Russell!"

The remarkable singing voice of Lillian Lewis, pealing from the choir in Dallas, where Russell was fulfilling a preaching

18

engagement, proved to be a siren call. She went as a bride to her new city, Galveston, where the family, as well as the groom, took her in. Cheerily she reported, "It was a lot of fun living with the Barbours." Russell's years with Lillian did much to exalt and enhance his life. Although no natural children blessed their marriage, two adopted youngsters graced the household: a son, now a medical technician, and a daughter, presently engaged as a primary school teacher.

Even though everybody loved Russell, it was clear that no one in the wide world did so more than Lillian. Her high dedication as a faithful wife and her pride at his remarkable attainment at such an early age of the pastorate of a good church assisted both in the realization of the work of their youthful dreams. Her admiration was captured by Russell's keen interest in the educational welfare of the young people of the church. After his passing, she said: "High school graduates, 'rare finds' in those days, were encouraged to attend college. Many were supported by scholarships and loans from the church. One of the young men was sent to Yale Divinity School; four to 'Big Ten' universities."

As beautiful as Galveston was as a living site, it had severe limitations for any who advocated civil rights. Poll taxes cursed the people. Lil's admiration for Russell must have grown as she observed his passion to lead out in the struggle for the racial justice which was denied to black people. The black church bore the brunt of the fight. From his stance as a pulpiteer, Lil's young husband parried the blows of the oppressors. "He cut his civil rights' teeth in the fight for voters' rights," were her proud words. Continuing, she said, "He always would read his sermons to me before preaching them." However, the manuscripts of his sermons are not available, a circumstance that is unfortunate for us.

The twofold burden of that pastorate was related to the problems that were spawned by the pulpit legacy left to him by his father and by his eight-year term as a bachelor pastor. Nevertheless, there were forces that served to give him solid support. There was the beneficial effect of mutual close association and intimacies shared in the marriage. Moreover, it is not trite to add that whatever further help was needed for the successful handling of problems was provided by his practice of daily prayer.

The fame of Russell Conwell Barbour relates directly to his association with his position as editor of *The National Baptist Voice*. He had had no special preparation for this calling; writers' conferences were not on the agenda of that day. By this time, Russell had become the pastor of the First Baptist Church of Nashville, Tennessee, now named the First Baptist Church, Capitol Hill. When the author was a ten-year-old boy, peddling the rival paper, *The Christian Review,* in the vestibule of his father's church, he even then knew of Barbour as the editor of *The National Baptist Voice.* In later years, he needed no eulogy or obituary to identify the great man.

Barbour's credentials, enhanced now by degrees from Morehouse and Colgate, plus an honorary degree from Bishop College, were further validated by the confidence of Lacy Kirk Williams, president of the National Baptist Convention, U.S.A., Incorporated, that the son of his old friend Alfred Barbour could handle the assignment. From 1930 until his death in 1944, Russell Conwell Barbour served in a manner that brought distinction to him and to the Convention and made a household word of his name throughout all the annals of the fellowship.

Not a few in the congregation at Nashville were unaware that Barbour's arrival was his way of using an opportunity to become the editor of *The Voice*. To a mutual friend, he is reported to have said, "Were there no *Voice,* there could be no meaningful response on my part to the challenge to live." Herein lies the tremendous vital thrust behind the work of this young minister. His persuasion that his denominational newspaper was the *élan vital* — the rationale for existence, the tonic for survival — knows few similar admissions among the confessions of pastors.

It is of utmost importance that this avenue of service, by virtue of its very uniqueness, caused his morale to skyrocket and made his job as a churchman more tolerable. As an employee of a black convention, performing such a unique, strategic, responsible task without relinquishing his pastoral and preaching duties, he became "number one" among many who coveted the prestige and power offered by such a position. It is not too important that, judged by strictest journalistic standards, he performed a mediocre task. He was a sensitive soul crying out under the crushing feeling of inadequacy. His position as editor compensated him for all of the shortcomings which might have disqualified him. How, then, did *The Voice* sustain Russell Conwell Barbour? By serving as a unifying force for the Convention and a liberating force for himself.

Physically small, his paper made him big. Although he was naturally even tempered and retiring, his typewriter made him like a man behind the wheel of a new car, changing him from a lamb into a lion, filling him with bold exhilaration. The nice, pacific guy then turned into an angry, needling news critic as, from this nonpulpit prodder's stance, he attempted to wake up the people. His better-than-average writing gift and his passion for hard work were tools sufficient to the task of erecting an eminence for the denomination and a place at the summit for himself as chief builder of good public relations for the four-million-member black organization.

His editorial writings in *The Voice,* unlike the meager sources of his sermons, are profuse. A careful review of such material impresses one that Russell Conwell Barbour was greater than his point of view. Despite the sharp shaft that was his pen, his temperament made him warm and friendly. While he was making enemies with his editorials, he was making a greater number of friends, who rushed to his side to fend off the poisonous barbs of angry detractors.

A fracas began when the editor included in the January 15, 1943, issue of *The Voice* an article entitled "I Ate Black-eyed Peas and Hog Jowl New Year's Day." In it he severely criticized conditions in Harlem and particularly excoriated the book by Adam Clayton Powell, Sr., entitled *Picketing Hell.* The response, a vitriolic hurricane of vituperative renunciation, all but blew the Convention apart. Powell's reply, "Editor Barbour and Rotten Hog Jowl," was published in *The National Baptist Voice,* March, 1943. One volley of the explosive content follows:

If one is to believe what appears on the front and fifth pages of the January 15, 1943 issue of the *National Baptist Voice,* Editor Barbour is on the danger list. His illness was caused by eating too much tainted hog jowl on New Year's Day. By a few strokes of his dyspeptic pen he relegates all Harlem Negroes in general and the Powells in particular to the ash-heap. The leading Negroes are a lot of windbags talking, bragging, and yelling instead of helping to feed and clothe the hungry, ragged maladjusted Negroes in the community. These Harlem colored are so terrible in looks and behavior that they not only make the city, for Barbour, the most depressing place in all his travels, but they forced John D. Rockefeller from their midst.

This outmuggs the white newspaper muggers. At last we have found a Negro newspaper monstrosity which warns people to keep out of Harlem unless they want to feel the awful weight of another depression.

By the time Editor Barbour reaches the fifth page, his hog jowl has given him acute indigestion. He tries to read my book, *Picketing Hell*, but temporary blindness caused by intense pain makes it impossible. He can't even see that it is a "fictitious novel" though that appears at the beginning of the book in bold black-face type. . . .

If Barbour is a gentleman, he will apologize in *The Voice* for this deliberate attempt to slander me. Until he does, he is the most unmitigated, malicious liar in the Negro pulpit. . . .

"If Barbour is a gentleman"? He was. Moreover, if he ever felt that it was appropriate to apologize, there is no record of it.

After this bitter scribal clash with the famous, highly respected New York pastor, there appeared an article in the April, 1943, issue of *The Voice* which had to be regarded as the prevailing view of most of the brethren touching the work of Editor Barbour. Written by M. S. Hunter of Albany, New York, it was entitled "Lest We Forget a Great Editor and a Great Paper: the Reverend R. C. Barbour and *The National Baptist Voice*." It contained these words:

> The editor [who] publishes on his front page articles of persons who criticize him because of his position on matters deserves praise. He is liberal and democratic, fair and honest, and keeps the columns of *The Voice* open to all. Editor Barbour does not consider anyone an enemy. He loves and respects all as friends.
>
> The harmony, goodwill, and spiritual unity of our National Baptist Convention, its Boards and Commissions are due in large way to the liberal, fair, and democratic editorial policy of our *National Baptist Voice*, as sustained by Editor Barbour. In the midst of the passionate storm and crisis through which we have passed we owe him words of praise.

Whatever Russell Barbour may have written that evoked the diatribe, it certainly was not characteristic of his actual nature. But it probably was in character with the peculiar air of tension of those days when personal striving exposed the sensitivities of proud and "touchy" men who had ascended to material heights without gaining a like spiritual eminence. The disease was an unsavory cultural malady incubated by jealousy and childish indulgence in creaturely self-love. To be sure, there were items upon which both parties were in total agreement, but no mention is made of them. In touching the sensitive nerve which set off such invectives, is it possible that Barbour succumbed to the temptation to thus test his editorial powers, asking no immunity from any onslaught which might follow a losing gamble?

Why did this altercation take place at all? If we probe the deep recesses of the speculative realm in searching for the reason, we may observe the human struggle for recognition and power, and the frantic flight from the obscurity of mediocrity, and assign these as motives. The whys and wherefores of black cultural behavior may provide the psychological answer.

Whenever Russell Conwell Barbour was overcome by spiritual despair, it was in part due to the suffering induced by an agonizing grief over the disunity of the brethren. With pen and voice, he poured out his life, attempting to stem the tide of dismemberment which was sweeping down upon his beloved church community. He craved the orderliness of the more peaceable kingdom when he sat in interracial fellowship in the caucus rooms of the publishing house. He joked editorially over the jocular, uninhibited jam sessions of his black brothers; but he soliloquized with sadness over the hard truth that his ethnic kin comprised a race but not a people. His resentment showed all through the telltale, murky sarcasm of his pages. With singular control over the myriad of his readers, his fingers fairly flew off in blind frenzy. He must have known the price he would have to pay for his unbridled indulgence in such delicious, sweet abandon, exploiting to the hilt his wanton editorial powers. Nevertheless, for the moment, the sheer exhilaration of it completely inundated his soul, fulfilled his spirit, sustained his days, enriched his life, and compensated thereby in some measure for that life's comparative brevity.

Meanwhile, the brutal fact that there remain three large black deliberating bodies incorporated as national Baptist conventions haunts the consciences of good men. The bizarre arithmetic of multiplying by dividing still frustrates, and the prospects of a retardation of the divisive process still seem to be exceedingly dim.

Barbour's dream was that his paper might be the glue which would unite the brethren. Challenged by this hope, he greedily embraced it until he became the incarnation of the unifying power which, in turn, fulfilled him and made him whole. Truly, he brought through his editorial effort a grandeur and stature to the National Baptist Convention, U.S.A., Incorporated, which it would have found difficult to attain otherwise.

THIRD TALENT

The trinity of gifts unfolds in full-orbed expression with the role of Russell Conwell Barbour as an educator. Perhaps there is less clarity in this area, but as professor of theology at the American Baptist Theological Seminary and chaplain of the Tennessee Agricultural and Industrial State University (now Tennessee State University), both at Nashville, the educational role may not necessarily be relegated to a minor classification. His previously mentioned philanthropies on behalf of his young people in the Galveston church and the influence of three colleges upon him further tend to qualify him.

No sparkling credentials were then a prerequisite to teaching at the seminary where, on a moonlighting basis, jobs were accepted not only to satisfy the teaching urge but also to provide a watershed for oneself in case a preaching ennui should ever require such insurance against ecclesiastical joblessness.

The catholicity of the ministry is one of its assets, but short-sighted congregations can neutralize the value of the pastor's possessions of a variety of skills by stultifying any thrusts not directed inwardly toward themselves. Civil responsibility and community involvement are barren of the influential presence of too many possible clerical benefactors by virture of the small-minded stance of otherworldly oriented church officials who regard religion strictly as an eschatological matter. They fail to see that where one goes in the hereafter depends upon what one goes after here. Hence, many pastors are held to the tether of ecclesiastical duty under their own vines and fig trees. The First Baptist Church, Nashville, was not peopled with such keepers of the house during the pastorate of Barbour, and neither is it under Kelly Miller Smith, its present pastor. It is a tribute to the membership that it recognized with an uncommon selflessness that a man's abundant resourcefulness cannot be contained in the routine busyness of parish duties. It must be released for the good of the commonweal through every possible channel leading to human enrichment and the improvement of the social order. Smith, as well as Barbour, taught at the American Baptist Theological Seminary. The key to the attractiveness of the Nashville church is doubtless the unique quality of its membership, renowned not so much because of the erudition which abounds, but because of willingness on the part of the congregation to share its leader.

CONSUMMATION

No prophetic insight was available to pierce the gloom of that melancholy afternoon when, on August 15, 1944, there gathered in the sanctuary of the First Baptist Church of Nashville the heaviest concentration of leadership from the National Baptist Convention, U.S.A., Incorporated, ever assembled outside of the actual meeting of the Convention itself. Around the mortal remains of Russell Conwell Barbour the cream of the black Baptist crop had gathered. Who, then and there, would have dared to suggest that within a decade a sickening fragmentation would have taken place? A newspaper account reports in a nostalgic manner of the small groups of people that gathered "here, there, and yon" on the outside of the church before the funeral services began. Where are the members of these groups today? Could they still meet, even under similar circumstances, at any common trysting place?

When the memorial service had begun, the master of ceremonies pleaded with the participants to spare the family by limiting their statements to three minutes. Who, indeed, has the magic words to heal this earth's breach of deadly separation, be they spoken in the space of three days, three hours, three minutes, or three seconds?

The death of Russell Barbour was a devastating blow to both friend and foe, but to his elder brother it was no less than a trauma. The hard anguish of it found its most agonizing expression in a brief but impassioned eulogy by "Joe" Pius. Recorded in *The Voice,* August 15, 1944, it was captioned "Well, Goodbye, Russell!" The polemics are shattering, underscoring with searing condemnation the folly of "pursuing the horizon" by ambitious men. *The Louisiana Advocate,* Baton Rouge, August, 1944, of which Gardner Taylor was editor, reported a similar lamentation entitled "Goodnight, Russell." This also displayed the understandable lachrymal outpourings of a devoted friend.

Four years later, during the sessions of the annual meetings of the National Baptist Convention, U.S.A., Incorporated, in Chicago, a sermon was preached by Russell's distraught friend Gardner Taylor. The address was entitled "It's Easter and Good Morning." It was gratifying to witness the resilience evidenced by rejection of the despair that had engulfed the fellowship four years earlier by the shock of Russell's death.

Out of the depths of their grief, the mourners at the memorial service overlooked the supreme opportunity of rejoicing at what God had been able to accomplish in so short a time through the life of Russell. Perhaps they should not have been expected under the circumstances to do so. But it should be pointed out somewhere, sometime, that the darkness of despair is always dynamited by hope and, in the light of the Christian faith, the goodbyes and goodnights will be replaced by "Welcome home!"

The eulogist for the memorial service was Marshall Shepard. *The Louisiana Advocate* had called him "one of the greatest extemporaneous preachers in America." With no announced subject, his point of departure was an appropriate Old Testament rendering of the last days of Israel's favorite son: "For David, after he had served his own generation by the will of God, fell on sleep" (Acts 13:36). Said one of the Convention leaders: "Shepard is fired by the great fellowship our crowd had known with Russell. He makes our burden lighter as he holds the visits of Grace before us."

Others added their testimonials to what Barbour meant to them. Helen (Dolly) Work who, as a youngster, enjoyed listening to him said, "He could squeeze every drop of substance from an idea." Coyness L. Ennix, a lifelong friend, said, "Russell sure could preach!"

Death, however, is not merely a leveler but a reconciler. Semantics can trick us if they fail to employ the essential perception to differentiate between "our crowd" and "the great fellowship." Is there any fellowship that is authentic if it is confined within the context of an isolated crowd? Rule by crony is neither new nor wholesome for the common good. William J. Simmons is chaplain at Tennessee State University, a post formerly held by Barbour. With reference to fellowship he says that an unseen but all-seeing television congregation, whose variety in terms of race, age, religion, and politics is lost in the unity which true worship provides, is caught up into the one great fellowship. Within such a context, it is reasonable to assume that the unlovely process of disintegration of the fellowship soon after the death of Russell Conwell Barbour was accelerated by his dreadful absence. How ironic it was that Russell's last sermon, "Out of the Depths," preached on August 4, 1944 — his attempt to extricate his hearers from divisiveness — was to be followed almost immediately by the advent of a dramatic deeper plunging return into the abyss and that his final overwritten editorial effort to rally a united march on Dallas presaged his own exalted entrance into the more "continuing city"!

EVALUATIONS

The time in which Russell Conwell Barbour lived was characterized by prolific pulpit sharing among the brethren. The tendency to gad about came naturally. Audiences were larger than congregations and, in spite of restricted travel conveniences, mobility marked the man who really knew how to preach. By such standards, Barbour was a world-beater. To sustain the loss of funds and prestige by refusing to take a series of "revivals" was not only unheard of, but also was thought to be downright indecent. These exchanges were guarantees of friendship and served when proffered as the imprimatur of being truly "in." The home congregations bore the brunt of the disarray brought on by such neglect in warmed-over sermons, the legacy of slovenly study habits, and the sloth induced by sheer fatigue. Relaxed moderation in eating, under the pressure of rival gustatorial temptations en route, took its toll. It seems significant that the record indicates that on the very day that Barbour was stricken — around noon — he had arrived in town at eight-thirty on that fateful morning from another appointment that had been a considerable distance away.

For a preacher to serve one charge for fifteen years, as Barbour did, is certainly commendable, but by black Baptist traditions this is of relatively short duration. In all probability, Russell's earthly journey was suddenly terminated by the contributing factor of these peripatetic excursions, not just around the nation but around the globe. Rather in endearment than in criticism, a fellow journalist, William A. Reed, Jr., wrote of him in a column called "The Voice of Today" (September, 1944):

> Now writer Barbour has written dispatches seated on a rock across from the site of Pilate's court in the Holy Land; has pulled out his notebook and written vivid impressions of spaghetti from Turin and Rome; and any American city with a hotel or YMCA is home to him.

The preacher, editor, and educator probably had no choice but to fall in line with his brethren. Who among them, given the same opportunities and blessed with such versatility, would not have moved about in similar fashion? If life begins at forty, he lived for about seven years. At the pace he chose to set for himself in obedience to the call of his vocational responsibilities, the miracle is that he should have lived so long.

In some ways, the First Baptist Church, Capitol Hill, Nashville, is a curious phenomenon. At first glance, to a minister, its attraction seems to be elusive, for it is not that of a mass membership nor a then impressive edifice. Anyone who seeks to shepherd her might be baffled if he tried to determine her worth by the usual criteria. Russell Conwell Barbour left a large parish in Texas to come to Nashville. Kelly Miller Smith, the present pastor, quickly returned to Nashville after a six-weeks' hiatus in Cleveland with one of Ohio's most prestigious congregations, preferring to resume his Nashville ministry, which now has stretched into twenty years. Could it be that a mission to restore the fellowship has been given by God as a charge to the remarkable people of First Baptist Church, Capitol Hill? Perhaps the burden to reconcile presses down upon the harried but willing shoulders of this prodigious group of people.

The conciliatory process that was begun when Barbour came to Nashville, and then fifteen years later was set aside, may well be the torch in the hands of Kelly Miller Smith as, in his inimical way, the ministry of sharing is deftly and creatively pursued by pastor and congregation.

The divisive elements which curse our times await the challenge of being matched by our healing ministries. If, like Russell Conwell Barbour, we perish with our swords still in our hands, we shall belong to a great company. If, given the opportunity, like Kelly Miller Smith, we continue to live with dreams of overcoming the tragedy of the unfulfilled with the glory of the attainable, Russell Conwell Barbour shall not have lived in vain. In seeking to establish unity among his brethren, Russell Conwell Barbour found his life. The rest of us remain in the wake of his untimely death.

James Timothy Boddie

An inadequate piano reeled under the amateur beat of stiff, untrained fingers, and a voice sang, "And I'm going there some day!" The player-singer was James Timothy Boddie, a preacher who was destined to go through life with a song in his heart.

Some score of years before, the epidemic that raged during the early years of the twentieth century had spared few babies, baring its fangs for a sharper bite into the black infant, as was its wont. There were grave doubts that little Tim, barely two years old, would make it through his bout with whooping cough.

Just at that time, Prophet Andrew Jones had come to Darby, Pennsylvania, on one of his annual preaching and healing revival missions. While there, he visited his friends, the Boddies, and found them frantically watching over little Tim. Of course, the prophet's prayers eased their minds. But, in addition, he pressed his mouth against Tim's, breathing deeply in and out in breath-giving and breath-taking cadence, just in time to prevent the child from slipping away. Known throughout the community, Prophet Jones, "the healer," had wrought another miracle! He had restored life to the lad even after he had been pronounced dead. It is doubtful if the healer had ever known about mouth-to-mouth resuscitation as it is known and practiced today.

BLESS THIS HOUSE

James Timothy Boddie was born in Darby on September 16, 1900, just as the twentieth century was also seeing the light of day. Tim's mother, Martha Branch Boddie, was sick and frail for most of her days, and soon after Tim's birth, she took her heavenly journey. She had a willing spirit but a weak constitution. The previous birth of Tim's sister Mary Frances, a precarious occurrence, was ill preparation for the more grim business of delivering Tim. The ordeal of giving birth to five children, of whom only Frances and Tim survived beyond infancy, abetted by the ravages of other ailments, proved to be too much for her.

It was apparent that another one was needed to give love and care in the Boddie household. The responsibility of homemaking fell upon the shoulders of Mary Gertrude Smith. After graduating from East Stroudsburg Teachers' College — the first of her race to do so — she married Tim's father and won her spurs not only as an ideal parent for the rugged preacher's two surviving offspring, but as the superb mother of those yet to be born. Under her competent supervision, Tim grew into a tall, gangling, self-conscious youth. Proud, yet mischievous, the entire neighborhood loved him and became, as it were, his family.

Perhaps because of the sacrifices that everyone had to make during World War I, he learned the lesson of thrift, a virtue which he nourished throughout all of his earthly days. A friend said, "When Tim let go of a penny, Abraham Lincoln stood up and stretched." No task was too menial for him to perform if it meant earning some extra change; he would shine shoes, sweep floors, or deliver papers. The school of all kinds of work established within him an independence that remained with him for life.

On June 25, 1928, Tim took Emery Moore from the organ bench in the Bethel Baptist Church, Brooklyn, New York, and married her. That she had been brought up in a parsonage made the union all the more effective, and she was to prove

to be an efficient minister's wife. The first three children arrived
on schedule: Marcia Lorraine, James Timothy, Jr., and Vashti
Ophelia. Then, after quite a time, Billy came along; he was
a surprise happening. All four of them are college graduates
and professional servants who are consistent followers of the
pattern set by the most venerable Boddie of them all, the father
of Tim, J. B. Boddie.

Marcia Lorraine, with daring and spunk that is not ordinarily
characteristic of her sex, worked with hardened gangs in the
Watts neighborhood of Los Angeles, one of the many areas in
America called cities, but whose more authentic designation
might rather be a sink of corruption. In an issue of *Time* about
three years ago, James Timothy Boddie, Jr., bore the honors
bestowed upon his brother black soldiers in Vietnam, where he
was an airman. Vashti Ophelia achieved the highest academic
honors on the baccalaureate and graduate levels at both Colby
and Cornell. William Leon, "Billy," who towers with Alcindor-
like grandeur above his peers, is a physician in Maryland. All
have families and all remember Papa with affection.

RISE UP, SHEPHERD

Tim instinctively knew that he was created for great things.
He had an early desire, an insistent obsession, to become a
preacher, like his father. Early, it was evident that he had the
necessary tools for the calling: an amazing spontaneity, a remarkable fluency, an uncanny dramatic flair, and an uncommon
gift for "imagineering." Coupled with these was an irrepressible
tendency to break out in song. His every gift was developed and
polished by his practice of preaching — with or without an
audience — in attic, basement, chicken coop, under the grape
arbor, and wherever and whenever he could. These youthful
sermons were always of the "whooping" kind, and their style
was never quenched by subsequent refinement.

When the time arrived for him to preach his first official
sermon, he chose the subject "Whom Seek Ye?" It was so well
done that he was awarded both a license to preach and ordination simultaneously, probably the first time this ever happened
in the annals of black Baptist history. The sermon was an
amazing production. Leaving nothing to chance, he used the

sermon as a medium to answer all the questions that he anticipated might be leveled at him by the ordination council. He
dispensed with every doctrinal item, from the Creation to the
Parousia, taking an hour in which to do it. When he had finished, it was considered that his handling of the theological
gamut was so comprehensive that the customary quiz was can-
celed. He was readily recommended for ordination, and the
meeting adjourned to an early chicken dinner. It mattered not
that his high school achievements were not up to a high academic
standard; in fact, the constant attention he had given to practice preaching under many conditions and circumstances paid
off.

Tim had been sure that it was right for him to lay aside all
secular tasks, be they his menial chores, a good job as a mail
clerk in Grand Central Station, New York, or his job as an
associate with Mr. Fields in the cleaning and dyeing business.
His ambition was to go to the seminary, where his father occupied a place on the board of directors. He had heard much about
President R. C. Woods and Vernon Johns, and he could hardly
wait to test his powers among such as they were.

In 1918, when he was licensed to preach by the Bethesda
Baptist Church, New Rochelle, New York, where his father
was the pastor, there were actually eight young men who answered the call to preach. The Bethesda Baptist Church sent
them all to Virginia Seminary and College, at Lynchburg, Virginia. Tim headed the phalanx. Undoubtedly the presence of
these men was the "shot in the arm" that has kept the venerable
institution going from that time until the present.

At Lynchburg, he found great satisfaction among a group
of like-minded students. For him, the atmosphere was relaxed
enough and the pattern casual enough for him to climb above
his peers scholastically and socially without effort. There were
two exceptions to this superiority: E. C. Smith rivaled him
academically, and John Williams, a close friend afterward,
showed him his social heels. To be sure, Tim's Lynchburg years
had made him a college-bred man, but now he yearned for
more education.

Although a graduate of Lynchburg was not a likely candidate
for admission to the stolid, stodgy, sophisticated Rochester Theo-

logical Seminary, Tim found himself ensconced therein in 1925. He served as president of the student body, and in 1928 he graduated. It was the year in which the Rochester Theological Seminary and the Religious Department of Colgate University merged to become the Colgate Rochester Divinity School.

At Rochester, Dr. George Cross and Professor Earle Bennett Cross, author of the Proverbs section of the *Abingdon Bible Commentary,* influenced Tim greatly. Between these two Crosses was Conrad Henry Moehlman, the noted church historian, whose inspiration moved Tim closer to being a scholar in his own right than he was ever to become. When he was president of the student body, he rubbed elbows with Albert Beaven and Clarence Barbour, between whom he sat. He had great admiration for George Ricker Berry and for Clarence Vichert, his friend and ethics professor. His closeness to all of these and to other inspiring professors made it only natural that he graduated with honors.

I CAN TELL THE WORLD

When the contentment of his decision to preach had fully settled within him, he developed ample sideburns around his full, round face. He glowed with the healthy assurance that he had made the only vocational choice possible for him if he were to attain full stature as the man he was destined to be. His blackness, accentuated with maturity, was regal. He needed no schooling in blackness and black pride. In truth, he embraced a race consciousness that was dangerously close to making him an anglophobe. Ivory white, clean, firm teeth were displayed almost consciously as a sign of his inner joy. His prominent lips were inclined to be full and smiling.

Like his father, Tim appeared to be big and strong. But his soul was so big that his 230-pound frame was scarcely big enough to contain it. But, paradoxically, his size did not support a deep, resonant, masculine voice that might have been expected. His voice was a staccato tenor, its stridency marked in song, and its hoarseness evident in every word. A chronic, throaty, almost gutteral pathological condition beset him. Listeners sympathized with him as the condition gradually worsened.

His straight, black hair was plastered down upon a well-shaped head. A telltale crease around the brow betrayed his meticulous attention to being well groomed. His dress and his car were also graciously subjected to scrupulous care. Jet-black eyes flanked his Roman nose — rare for one of his race — and his lips would protrude when he was deep in thought or reverie. His furrowed brow triggered an automatic pucker of his mouth.

His laugh was gigglish, high, and falsetto; it was more pleasant to see than to hear. "Isn't that funny, Mamma?" he would ask his wife. Then away he went into his chuckle, whether it was evoked by some ancient bit from "Amos and Andy" or by the sophisticated quip of a wise news commentator.

Through the years, any event or circumstance that struck him as being significant or interesting brought forth his oft-repeated expression: "That's powerful!" These words were usually whispered, not shouted. The high tribute was character-istically paid to events which ranged from aesthetic pleasures to intellectual profundities, from banal trivialities to earth-shaking revelations. All such were vaulted to supreme signifi-cance by Tim's magnificent accolade: "That's powerful!" always whispered hoarsely. A toothsome meal produced by the skilled culinary hand of Emery would cause him to purr in a com-pletely relaxed half moan and half tone another expression of his own: "Mamma, that was *together!*"

Spiritually powerful sermons gushed in sluices from this great reservoir. He was a dynamo of energy, whose utterances for forty years inspired great congregations and countless audiences all over the country. He was preacher, revivalist, and songster.

After his fiftieth birthday, he began to know a lassitude in which the agility of earlier years waned. Overweight, which ever plagued his adulthood, seemed to defy control. Sometimes he could be heard humming to himself while shuffling phantom-like through the second floor of his apartment at 821 Lanvale Street, Baltimore.

I'M A-ROLLING

The first pastorate of the Reverend James Timothy Boddie was at Lackawanna, New York. It was a real "pressure cooker." Sheer preaching prowess carried him through three precarious years. In 1931 he was called to the Union Baptist Church, Baltimore. This very aristocratic church was known for the presence in its membership of many college-trained constituents, a rare circumstance at this time. This urban haven for the black bourgeois did not match too well with the whirlwind preaching style of the preacher-songster, so again he set off to what was then a suburban charge in Germantown, in the northwestern section of Philadelphia, Pennsylvania, where he became the pastor of the Mount Zion Baptist Church. However, this church was able to hold him for only three years.

Upon the death of Dr. Whitt Allen, pastor of the New Shiloh Baptist Church, Baltimore, Maryland, Tim received an invitation from the pulpit committee to become a candidate for that vacant pulpit. On one Wednesday night, he literally sped to Baltimore and preached the congregation "plumb out of its skin"; he turned the place "out." Called by the New Shiloh Baptist Church, he accepted the pastorate with relish, passion, and nostalgia. A Baltimore church with soul was his dream. And he would exert a pastoral responsibility that would raise it to its highest effectiveness. Tim and that church must have been right for each other, for he stayed there for twenty-one years until his translation.

New Shiloh was a porridge that tasted just right. It was large, prestigious, relaxed, free-wheeling, emotional, and intellectual; all colors of the spectrum were reflected from the most hetero-geneous homogeneity imaginable. By contrast, the Union Baptist Church of that city maintained a formality that irked him. This he could handle well enough, but his heart was not in it. That charge had been a pleasure but not a challenge such as New Shiloh presented. In his latest church, he was a commoner, but he could act like an aristocrat. He could wear a pulpit gown or leave it hanging in the closet. He wore it. While preaching, he avoided habit-forming behavior patterns. If every movement had a meaning all its own, he made every meaning possess a move-ment all its own. His choirs became proficient in every kind of church music, from anthems to soul music. All tastes, from those of youth to those of old age, were satisfied. All occasions were covered, from festival to funeral, and from traditional worship to special occasions. The reason Shiloh acquired a "grieving choir" for funerals only after the Second Baptist

Church, Los Angeles, already had one was that Shiloh did not think of it first.

Those who are unfamiliar with the black church lack the understanding and appreciation of what the board of ushers means. If the choir may be called the war department, the board of ushers should be called the glory department. All other church auxiliaries and organizations pale in the wake and backwash of the swashbuckling, intense, dynamic stride of this virile group, whose uniforms, manners, decor, and military precision are reminiscent of the old pompous Marcus Garvey festivals.

These prestigious ushers' organizations are more difficult to "crash" than an exclusive campus fraternity ball. When it is learned that some such boards, divided into sexes, are impressive enough in dimension to have choirs as adjuncts within their very organizational structures, one begins to grasp the idea. New Shiloh was no exception. All events sponsored by the usher boards reeked with bigness, pageantry, formality, and collections. Extreme formalism, replete with signals from the captain, to the lieutenants, to the pawns marked each worship service. Then the announcement of the text of the day indicated the time for all ranks to retreat, formally but surreptitiously, to the obscurity of the cloistered rear pews, for as the preacher took over, the ushers would not begrudge him the time-honored and hard-won limelight.

Reminders of antebellum times, when men and women were separated by something other than sex, were the monetary assessments exacted by the ushers at collection time: one dollar from the men, and fifty cents from the women. This practice accentuated the real or imagined superiority of the male. Further embellishments in stewardship were added by means of penny offerings and consecrated dimes from everyone. Thus, mission giving is scant where stewardship education is largely unknown. Nevertheless, every piece of the coin of the realm, from a penny to a five-dollar bill (rarely seen), was gathered with as much ceremony as the dispensation of the Communion service. Pomposity, circumstantial reverence, and heightened conspicuousness enriched the pot and lifted the morale.

Tim's church was arrayed with the grandest of boards of ushers conceivable in a black church. And he reveled in it.

Few pulpiteers could tell the story as he. The late C. T. Epps, Sr., after hearing him preach in Boston for the New England Baptist Convention, exclaimed, "The man was born to preach!" Tim was! And Tim knew it. The reality of his call sustained him, and he was lost in its exacting commitment. All of the morbidity, dullness, and dailiness of the week was transfigured in his zeal, his single-minded purpose, and the life-exuding experience of his spirit which no word can describe. Here, in a pulpit, surrounded by three choirs, with another one in the front balcony, and a crowded sanctuary of a thousand people, now stood an authentic purveyor of the Word. He never preached other than a great sermon.

Never, from his first pastorate in Lackawanna to his fourth and last one in the New Shiloh Baptist Church, did his listeners lack for a powerful message. Tim could, and did, preach like his father, a fact which sustained him throughout his ministry. That he understood and knew this truth warmed the cockles of his heart and gave every Sunday a special significance to him.

Inherently he had a flair for the dramatic, somewhat tempered by his deep reverence and respect for his elders. As a lad, he had indulged in a moving-picture enterprise, both as viewer and producer, charging a penny a show. Like Barnum, he was a born showman, if not sometimes a downright ham. Also there was more than a little gypsy in him, for he liked to travel. Although his trips were not as frequent as those of his father, they were more far-flung. For example, in 1954, when the Baptist World Alliance met in London, he was there, making a European jaunt.

But of all days, Sunday was his day. When it arrived, he came alive. Aroused by its necessities and spurred on by the lift of family worship, he feasted not only upon the gustatorial morsels prepared by the culinary skill of his wonderful wife, but also upon his regard for the day. The week's most important day found him to be a sermonic dynamo, a reservoir of spiritual power and prophetic utterance, God's ramrod.

STEAL AWAY

It was Tim's literal wish that he might die in the pulpit. How gratified he would have been if he might have known his New

Shiloh's praying and preaching ground as the Mount Pisgah's lofty height from whence he could have viewed his home and taken his flight! But his heavenly Father had another ingenious plan for securing his memory.

Stubbornly, if not wisely, he felt sure of his ability to abort the ravages of diabetes, but his great strength buckled under the weekly strain, further sapped by too-frequent vigorous preaching engagements both at home and abroad. Telltale signs began to appear: the short breath, the wide gape of dry mouth, the hoarseness, the futile efforts to wring from tired vocal cords the once bell-like strident tone, the new brevity that, for him, was so uncharacteristic, and the abrupt, nonclimactic conclusions to sermons. All these presaged the near end of the valiant fight for another soldier of the cross.

It will long be remembered that about one o'clock on the afternoon of November 22, 1963, shots rang out in Dallas, Texas, and John Fitzgerald Kennedy left the scenes of this world. Only about three hours later, and without knowledge of that event, James Timothy Boddie went home to his Maker. On the same day, James and John had gotten together. Like his father, Tim had shortened his life by his strenuous, all-out preaching exertions.

Back in the Bethesda Baptist Church, in New Rochelle, no Communion service would close when J. B. Boddie was the pastor without congregational participation in the song "This May Be My Last Time." One rhyming couplet in the song goes:

> Old Death can't make my soul afraid;
> I don't mind old death no more'n I do my "baid!"

He didn't. Nor did Tim.

The song that Tim had sung so often, "And I'm Going There, Some Day," was sung again at his funeral by Mrs. Margaret McRae, of the Union Baptist Church, where he had once served as pastor. "He killed himself for us," wailed Dr. Lillie Jackson, leader of the National Association for the Advancement of Colored People. Mrs. Verda Welcome, a state senator, expressed similar sentiments. All the members of the clergy, including his special friend Rolland Dutton, his Caucasian roommate at the seminary, paid tribute for a life that had been literally poured

40

out for others, even as his Master had emptied himself. All of these loved and admired Tim.

After the eulogy, delivered by Tim's friend A. J. Payne, Theodore McKeldin, former governor of Maryland and then mayor of Baltimore, paid his tribute. Tim had prayed during the governor's inauguration at Annapolis. At the pastor's and Mrs. Boddie's twenty-fifth wedding anniversary, Mr. and Mrs. McKeldin were honored guests, and they remained until the very end of a long, heat-generating affair. On any Sunday, the governor could be seen in a back pew after "sneaking in," as it were, to hear his favorite preacher. Now His Honor had highlighted the funeral service by his auspicious presence and his emotional statement. If anyone should be interested in learning how to increase that harvest which reconcilement brings, he would do well to ponder the Christlike affinity which bound these two men in thralldom to the very end.

The surviving preacher brothers assisted at the obsequies and, with the rest of the brothers and their nephews (Tim's sons), became active pallbearers. The women wept, but the tears they shed were not those of despair. Nostalgic joy, perhaps inspired by the theme of one of his favorite hymns, "Come, Thou Fount of Every Blessing," assured them that the "courts above" had received a royal son and subject.

This was no small wonder, for he had sung repeatedly "And I'm going there some day!"

JUST LIKE J. B.

To think of Tim is to think of his father, Jacob Benjamin Boddie. Both were great preachers. Both married worthy helpmates. Both educated their children. Both were constantly in great demand and found their audiences larger than their congregations, which were huge. Born to preach, both were the victims of calendars that were too full for their physical capacities. Both were spiritual giants whose lengthy lists of converts in their evangelistic enterprises were about even.

There was no escaping notice of the mutual pride each held for the other. Tim idolized his father; J. B. was expansively proud of his son. Such mutual respect was an incentive to keep both at their preaching best. Central in black worship is preaching, and they both knew it. Therefore, pride of profession, as well as their instinctive rivalry, goaded them ever to greater heights. The father's excellence was produced by the intuitive knowledge which he brought to the task; the son's high-quality performance was the result of preparation and natural ability.

The results of their labors were sweeping and lasting. If totaled, converts from their revival efforts would form an impressive congregation. Tim was a great preacher; his father greater. Perhaps the reason was that the old man had "a way with his feet." No such unorthodoxies accompanied Tim's delivery. Tim, who was a man as clean as a hound's tooth, justified his every sermon with his own life ingredient, character. Yet, of his father it was said, "He is the greatest character-building preacher his day has known." Tim, the master homiletician and expositor, found his father's preaching to be so dynamic that folks could not stand it. In C. E. Boddie's book *Giant in the Earth*, Adam Clayton Powell, Sr., said in his Foreword that the father was the greatest preacher of his time that the race has produced. Tim, a singer and physically impressive in the pulpit, had to step aside for this giant in the earth, his father, who was truly without peer.

Tim had soul power, charisma; but the father had more, plus wisdom. Tim leaned toward caution; the father had a "go for broke" abandon about him, betting his life that his dedication would find God standing in the shadow keeping watch above his own. Tim sank resignedly and enjoyably into the plush seat of the comfortable. Tim moved only if he was sure that the next step would solidly support him, wearing well the coat of conformity; his father was forever "tearing up the pea patch." Tim, the more stolid, accepted but did not fully embrace the humorous venture as a technique in his preaching; the father found humor to be one of the most effective arrows in his sheaf. Tim was very conscious of Tim, having only a scantling of humility; the father, a physical powerhouse, was, at the same time, a child in the Father's hands. The cross was a ready symbol for sermon and song for the son; for the father, it was that to which he constantly bore witness.

Tim's relationship with white people rested at one time upon a very slender reed, but roommates at the seminary got him over that hump. The father knew no shred of racism; he had been schooled in openness of mind and heart by a virtual college education at the hands of Caucasian theologians and churchmen who spiritually filled him at the Northfield Summer General Conferences.

Many cultural media were available to Tim, providing him with a link to the world; no such tools were in the cache of the tenant-farm-born father. The urban setting molded the mind-set of the younger; bare feet in red sod supported the youthful J. B. Boddie. Four children sprang from the union of Tim and Em; twenty saw the light of day from the union of two spouses with the father. Annual reports came out in easy prose from the pen of the son; the father decked out his reports in Isaac Watts' style common-meter rhyme. They said that Tim was a man who preached like his father; they called the older man "Black Billy Sunday." The son required the vigorous boost that education could give him; the father dropped out at the end of the sixth grade. Tim's automobiles were big, sleek, and shiny; the father rode in a car that cost five dollars and had to be stopped every ten miles for water.

Obviously, there could have been no Tim without J. B. The family reunions which take place every three years are meaningful especially because of the father. Tim would be the first to recognize this fact and glory in it. The rest of the family follows in respecting their heritage.

BREAK BREAD TOGETHER

In spite of the fact that Tim had a bad case of racial "measles" during his youth, he swung completely around to the opposite attitude and ended his career within the strong fellowship of white Baptists. Strife among the black Baptist conventions was so sharp that he suffered a trauma that resulted in his complete withdrawal from black convention alliance. He regretfully did so, even though he had served on the national level as an officer and on the state level as president. His syndrome was relieved as he returned to activity, now with American Baptists. Although he never reached the point wherein he lost all race consciousness, his barbs were much less sharp than had been his tirades against Caucasian injustice. Still changing as his involvement with

American Baptists increased, his usefulness as a reconciler was just about to be tapped when God took him.

His great friendship with Martin Luther King, Sr., put him within easy reach of the tide-sweeping influence of the more famous son. Tim's wife, Emery, a Spelman College classmate of Martin Luther King, Jr.'s, mother, helped to deepen his total involvement. The American Baptist Assembly at Green Lake and the annual Convention sessions of American Baptists found him conspicuously placed, especially in the Christian Education Week sessions. He served as an important member of a then new feature in the American Baptist Convention called the Caucus representing the American Baptist Churches in the South.

When Tim's father passed on, Tim felt that, in the light of the mores that then were becoming current, "Papa went just in time." But toward his last days, he himself was found to chafe with embarrassment at the "new morality," which he, along with Billy Graham, was wont to call "the old immorality." Perhaps he, too, went just in time.

Ernest Coble Estell

To the stunned millions watching prime-time television, a little giant named Ernest Coble Estell disdained using the whitewash brush that seemed to have been passed to him, and he minced no words in exposing a national tragedy for what it was. Only two days before, on Friday, November 22, 1963, the nation's youthful President John Fitzgerald Kennedy had been assassinated. With this shot, the nation's slumber also had been shattered. The city of Dallas, under the sting and shock of sudden disgrace, was, to many minds, endeavoring to exonerate itself before the nation. Before the numberless citizenry watching the TV screen from coast to coast and border to border, participants in a handpicked coterie of the cream of the city fathers of Dallas were attempting to restore the city's fractured image. The first speakers on the panel included the president of the chamber of commerce, a Roman Catholic priest, a white Protestant clergyman, and a Jewish rabbi.

Then Ernest Coble Estell spoke.

Instead of taking his cue from the tawdry attempts at explanation offered by his predecessors in that sordid episode, he caused the broadcast to spring to life with a frank, searing, pene-

47

trating condemnation of the known pockets of hate from which was born the spark that triggered the dastardly deed. His mien and message carried an authenticity which injected spine and teeth into that television program.

This was not the time for a painful recitation of spurious rationalizations or a conjuring up of excuses for human frailty whereby a broken people would be left to languish in the treacherous quicksands of false hopes. Only an unvarnished confession could have redeemed the awful moment. Only a drawing back of the curtain revealing the bleak drama of the naked, raw, insidious barbarisms that lurk in the human breast could have satisfied the severe requirements of surviving that dreadful experience. Of those selected to appear on the telecast to try to save the face of the metropolis in its heartrending hour, only the black preacher, in apparent defiance of the wishes of those around him, offered up himself to stave off the demons of utter despair by his unashamed facing of the cameras in honest contrition. His contribution was a straightforward acknowledgment of the horrible hostility that killed the young leader and shocked the nation. He made it in an unabashed, well-articulated, and sober public exposure which helped to set the record straight. He made no brazen attempt to restore a tarnished image or to explain away the heinous deed. If the tragic death of John Fitzgerald Kennedy accomplished naught else, it revealed the solid worth of Ernest Coble Estell, who secured his position of greatness by the unequivocal stand he had taken.

WINSOME LITTLE GIANT

Owlish, Eddie Cantor-like orbs bulged out of a near-grotesque forehead, almost making Ernest appear to be glowering. These were assembled over prominent, but loosely pursed, full lips, casually set over a chin that had a trace of a dimple. He had a full-blown, brown face, flanked by a pair of outsized ears. His spare, short, stocky frame, arched by yoke-like shoulders, embraced a well-stacked torso. All these domiciled the stout heart of a character who possessed an abundance of poise, dignity, courtesy, and gentility.

This bantam rooster of a man, appropriately topped with a smooth cockscomb, often tightly plastered down, knew how to laugh his way through life and into the affections of his fellowmen. He was always nattily attired and well groomed.

Robert Cole Estell and his wife, Sarah, lived in Decherd, Tennessee. They were the parents of three sons, of whom Ernest Coble was the eldest, born on January 12, 1894. During a revival meeting in the Baptist Church of Decherd, Ernest accepted Christ and was baptized. As a young man, he went to St. Louis, where he fell in love with Miss Leona Casey and married her. Eventually nine children were born of this happy union.

Some time after Ernest was already a father, he heard and answered the call to the ministry. He was then a member of the First Baptist Church of St. Louis, where O. Clay Maxwell was the pastor. His education after his public schooling in Decherd was graduation from the Summit High School in St. Louis, courses in the Alabama A. & M. College, and graduation from Simmons University, Louisville, Kentucky, where he received the B.Th. degree. His later activities brought him collegiate honors in the form of the Doctor of Divinity degree from Simmons University, and both the Doctor of Distinguished Service and Doctor of Law degrees from Bishop College.

Too numerous to mention are the many responsibilities and positions of leadership which he held. These took him into the work of the Boy Scouts of America, the YMCA, community organizations, interracial organizations, interdenominational organizations, Negro societies, every level of Baptist denominational work, college trusteeship, high offices in fraternal organizations, positions in city government, and membership in the president's Committee on Civil Rights.

One day it became a part of God's plan for him to bid farewell to Leona, his first love. For a time there was solitude in the home, but he realized that it is not good for man to live alone. Therefore, in 1930, he married Miss Lee Ella Payne, of Owensboro, Kentucky. This fine woman became his constant companion, an inspiration to him in the work of the ministry, and a capable mother for his children.

HOW TO LIVE

"I have learned how to live, I have learned how to be sick,

and I have learned how to die," wrote Estell. Somehow the expression strikes one as being artificially put together, as some deathbed, pontifical statement might be. Perhaps Estell, after years of sermonizing, instinctively strove for some sort of rhythm of expression and, in so doing, got involved in a clumsiness of word use. In the name of needed clarity, can we probe further into his possible intention?

First, let us add a fourth statement: "I have learned how to stay well." To this, let us affix a fifth thought: "I have learned how to adjust to lingering illness." To know how to stay well and then to learn how to adjust to illness if and when it befalls is the sign of a mature person.

"I have learned how to live," he proclaimed. He ably demonstrated this truth on the night of November 24, 1963, when he spoke to the nation. The discipline, obedience, and fearlessness issuing from that well-ordered life filled the emptiness of that melancholy night with hallowed light. He had learned how to stay well—how to live—and his grasp on the gift of precious health enabled him to take his forthright stand.

Then, too, to learn how to stay well is an essential endowment if one successfully lives out, as did Estell, such a fruitful and action-packed ministry, capped by a wizardry in business affairs and an expertise in combining religious and secular operations into amazingly successful enterprises for the good of the commonweal. The added grace of health was surely needed to preserve his role in the art of parleying unlikely combinations into rewarding cadres that would have purpose and worth. And at this kind of activity, he was a past master.

After his call to the ministry, he was called to the pulpit of the Bethel Baptist Church, of Drakesboro, Kentucky. In 1927 he moved into the pastorate of the Tabernacle Baptist Church, of Dayton, Ohio, where for ten years he spent an energetic and sensational ministry. Hearing of such success, the St. John Baptist Church, of Dallas, Texas, sought him for the pastorate of that great church. Reminiscent of the bold and fearless One who "must needs go through Samaria," this prophet's opened door compelled him to go through Texas, scorning the consequences and the adverse advice of friends and kindred.

Truly he had learned how to live! The work in Dallas was

taxing, but exhilarating. Arriving in Dallas on January 1, 1938, he was to see the erection of a new, larger building in three years. It seems almost unbelievable that he once baptized 190 candidates in a single ceremony. It is of little wonder, therefore, that he ultimately had a membership of four thousand at St. John Baptist Church.

The church was, indeed, a beehive of activity. To man the profuse ecclesiastical establishment, he engaged the hands of the members themselves and trained them through whatever means of leadership resources were at his disposal. His organizational genius showed itself in the operation of a full-time institutional program; Sunday worship was only one of many functions in the total business of personal development and fulfillment for his people and himself. No ministry of helpfulness was deemed irrelevant; the church's services included such unchurchly ministries as banking through cooperative savings and involvement in a real estate business.

A similar application of his all-pervading ministry was released upon every community organization in which he took a part. Introducing innovations not seen or heard of previously in place of the stodginess produced by blind habit caused him to be surrounded by a fraternal glow. His concern for and interest in young people found their high point in his work with the National Baptist Sunday School and Training Union Congress. As a result of his input of time, money, and personal leadership as vice-president, the congress reached a numerical delegate strength that was equal to that of the National Baptist Convention, U.S.A., Incorporated, itself.

Coincidentally, it seemed that Ernest Coble Estell reached the zenith of his brightness upon the darkest days of infamy. His appearance on the national network of television stations revealed him as standing for truth and frankness when others were temporizing. The first occupation of the new building of the St. John Baptist Church, at Allen and Guillot Streets, Dallas, Texas, had taken place on another calamitous day—Pearl Harbor Sunday, December 7, 1941. Perhaps the congregation had had occasion to forget Pearl Harbor and to remember St. John! The battler-preacher had symbolized the pathos of those tragically memorable days.

Outside the church, he carried other responsible commitments. He was devoted to the National Baptist Convention, U.S.A., Incorporated, in which he served as a member of the executive board and as vice-president of its Sunday School and Baptist Training Union Congress. His relations with the president of the Convention were those that paid high regard for the one whose office was to be respected. In every area of service, he displayed a sincere loyalty to Jesus Christ and to the ideals of the organization and the people who served by his side. Nothing remained in the realm of negligence to clobber his sense of self-esteem. He wore well, pondered long, thought keenly, and responded definitely.

Two evidences demonstrate that he had learned how to live — to stay well. Once he bounded into a taxicab; then he discovered that there was another gentleman who also was looking for such a conveyance, and he invited him to ride along. Throughout the ride, Estell's conversation rolled along unrelentingly, filled with jolly, cryptic loquacity. At the end of the ride, over his companion's not too insistent demurrer, he paid the fare for both and bade his new friend Godspeed. The second illustration of his abounding health is to be found in his preaching style. He was always prancing as though he were one of "seven lords a-leaping," presumably compensating for his lack of physical height, especially if he happened to be preaching in the presence of associates who might easily have lost him in the tall timber of their own physically towering adjacency.

ROBUST PREACHER

If greatness can rightly be appended to a description of the preaching of Ernest Estell, it is because of its evangelistic content. He went after sinners. He would be the first to admit that his education was not extensive enough to cause reverberations throughout the intellectual community and campus environs as would the thunderous, prolific perorations of a Vernon Johns. But the common man heard him gladly, and the results speak for themselves. With the speed and profusion of a cyclonic sweep, names were added to the membership rolls of the churches which he served. The Tabernacle Baptist Church, of Dayton, Ohio, underwent embarrassing episodes, experienced irritating incidents which all but demeaned her out of existence, and suffered the ignominious chagrin of debilitating litigation and hostility. Nevertheless, all of these impedimenta were sloughed off, and the church rose to great numerical and spiritual heights under Estell's preaching. The enemies of the church smacked their lips, awaiting in vain to celebrate the "descent into Hades" of the alleged saints in that smitten household. But no such thing happened, because of the impact that the life of this man had upon the entire black community as he fought off the Sanballats and rebuilt the walls of confidence which surrounded the Tabernacle family, for he had the tenacity and resourcefulness of a Nehemiah. His elixir of evangelistic passion was one of the potent ingredients in the restorative potion that forestalled the demise of the church. His ministry of healing such breaches attracted the attention of all of the black Baptists of the city. By Estell's persuasive hand they continued to be led. This mighty preacher of rare power entertained a passion for salvation for them that turned them on spiritually.

An example of his preaching prowess can be seen in the sermon which he delivered at Hot Springs, Arkansas, to a large gathering of fellow Baptists who were holding a conference related to denominational business. Even when he preached to this group, the evangelistic elements were clear and prominent. The subject was "Don't Let Them Get You Down!" It was bolstered by the text taken from the Moffatt translation of Mark 15:32: "Come down now from the cross! Let us see that and we'll believe!" When he confessed to those close by "I have learned how to die," the secret of how he came by such empowerment was disclosed.

In this Calvary-centered homily, the dying Lord, atoning for human sin, is at the apex of a soteriological pyramid firmly held together by the mortar of sound gospel preaching and an enthusiastic outpouring of the unction of biblical revelation. These principal ingredients were augmented in their effectiveness by the usual presence in the exhortation of Estell's charisma and soul. Indeed, this sermon had aspects of a pep talk addressed to preachers who were on the verge of apostasy. Estell sensed their need for a firing up to a fresh dedication if they were to be able to meet the requirements of the times to witness relevantly as true servants of that Christ "who refused to come down." With their beloved Lord, who continued to hang rather than respond to the taunts of the crowd to have it otherwise, they, too, were warned to remain and refuse to come down. Remembering not only who, but also whose, they were, they were urged to follow the example of fortitude and courage that was so redemptively and passionately unfolding upon that tree. Although it is not certain that his admonition was wholeheartedly welcomed, it cannot be gainsaid that his entreaty was solidly reinforced with exceptional vigor and exuberance of lung power.

Although much may be lost in reading such a sermon, it requires only a trace of imagination by the initiated to identify the locations which could be filled only by charisma during the actual preaching. That Ernest Coble Estell was amply endowed with the necessary equipment to enhance the presentation at such times was recognized by those who were in the room then, and by all who knew the veteran preacher.

Five times, the projection of the familiar scene at the foot of the cross was punctuated by the all-compulsive counterblast: "There is too much involved!" The derisive, taunting crowd mockingly shouted at the Crucified to "come down!" Increasing the intensity of his utterance each time, again and again he cried, "There is too much involved!" This, he offered, was the basic reason for Christ's refusal to come down. Although the preacher did not elaborate upon what aspects in their involvement would be risked or destroyed by their coming down, or what it was that would be forever lost by such a move, not one person present could escape the force of the blast delivered by the ever-increasing escalation of the plea.

He cited the danger of preaching so prophetic a gospel as to make the foes of justice and racial equality tremble. He predicted persecution, perhaps martyrdom, for those who would persist, whether they be in the North or the South, in "rocking the boat." But whatever their respective fates might be for taking their fearless stand, he shouted his encouragement to colleagues who might be "on the ropes" for their heroics and their complacency-shaking utterances, again urging them not to "come down," even though to remain steadfast would place their very lives in jeopardy. "The Master did not come down!" he repeated. "You must not come down! There is too much involved!"

There was a relationship between this great evangelistic sermon and the occasion when the man sat before the gaze of millions, dynamiting the darkness of a dreary national episode. Practicing on that eerie November night in Dallas the thing that he had preached on a cold January day in Hot Springs, he allowed no one to get him down. There was too much involved!

Salvation is a grace that is not only bestowed. Salvation is also created. To illustrate this point, Estell took an existing song, "The Lord Will Make a Way Somehow," and added the words, "So can I." With the Lord's help, he succeeded in doing so. As what has been called his crowning achievement, he executed the building of luxury-housing units under the auspices of his church. Today the three-million-dollar housing project, bearing the name Estell Village, indicates his concept of the kind of salvation that is created on behalf of those who, bereft of freedom of access because of their race, had, nevertheless, to live somewhere. His refusal to allow his people to be forced to make any old, shabby habitat do, and their rallying around the pastor, who led them to living quarters that would enhance their dignity and self-esteem, are things of beauty and a joy forever. Estell shared the philosophy of Adam Clayton Powell, Jr., who said, "Golden slippers there and leather shoes here; mansions in the sky there and good housing here." This "salvation *is* created."

Estell's achievement in creating salvation in the form of good housing was the forerunner of more notable achievements that were to be made. Some of these, to be seen today, are the Opportunities Industrialization Centers, church cooperatives, credit unions, and real estate enterprises of various magnitudes with government aid. Such projects are successfully being carried on in not a few contemporary black church settings throughout the United States. If this be black power, so be it, and more power to it!

The quality of Estell's performance was guaranteed by the sensitivity which he felt in this arena of pastoral leadership. No ragtag housing would do. His approach displayed a wily business acumen. In this, and in all matters touching the lives of his parishioners, he moved with the sophistry that belied the etiology of a legacy inherited from a tradition which once knew slavery. His crowning achievement caused his people to raise their Ebenezers of praise by the investiture of a permanent memorial in the form of giving his name to the entire project. The St. John Luxury Apartments near Bishop College, which he insisted must really be luxurious, were renamed "Estell Village," and this whole project stands today as an added monument to the great church which he had served, and to his own glorious memory.

The following words by Manual L. Scott, printed in his pamphlet "Dr. Ernest C. Estell and Estell Village (Highland Village Project, Charitable Foundation)," were expressed on the occasion of the dedication:

> When the pains and pathos of poor housing humiliate and agonize persons and people; whenever overcrowdedness obstructs the freedom so necessary to families for self fulfillment; whenever the sight of slums which breed ill health and unhappiness makes us sick with pity; whenever the clamor and cry for governmental assistance is heard; and whenever the disinherited hunger and thirst after better tabernacles for their bodies, Estell Village serves as a monumental reminder to the churches that they have the opportunity and obligation to help.

The author of the foregoing quotation had not completed his tribute before death overtook the hero of the drama. This intervention on the part of the Rider on the Pale Horse contributed as much to the impetus which brought about the changing of the name as the incessant pressure from Ernest Estell's admirers to impose the new nomenclature.

HOW TO ADJUST

"I have learned how to be sick," he had written; and our conjecture is that he could rather have said, "I have learned how to adjust to lingering illness." The normal ways of human flesh ordained that the time must come when he would need to call upon this phase of his philosophy. The illness appeared; and it lingered. He suffered excruciatingly. When he was called on the telephone one day, his voice was unrecognizably weak; so much so that it revealed the closeness of the end. Nevertheless, it was a sure thing that he was moving out uncomplainingly, banners flying, unsheathed sword pointing toward the City of Hope, even as he was gradually falling beneath the frightful weight of the trial of affliction. He had learned indeed.

The author confesses that he is the one who made that telephone call on that hot day in Dallas. The remainder of his journey to Glorieta, New Mexico, became more tolerable because of a sick man's encouraging word, and the humid heaviness pressing down from a brassy sky became more bearable. Although Estell had great devotion to Bishop College and took pride in having earned his diploma from Simmons University, and in spite of his distracting illness, he chose the time and the circumstance of the telephone conversation to inquire about the welfare of the American Baptist Seminary, at Nashville. His uplifting and cheering conversation, happily carried on despite the interruption of his Sunday meal, somehow made a rugged ordeal on the airline's "mountain yoyo" entirely worthwhile. In his state of severe bodily illness, he more than matched with his own the comfort coming to him from his healthier brother on the opposite end of the telephone line. He had learned how to be sick.

HOW TO DIE

He had said it: "I have learned how to die." It was the concluding part of his little trilogy. Here, we may call upon the black bards of long ago to help with an interpretation of what Estell meant. The spiritual goes:

> I want to die "easy" when I die,
> I want to die "easy" when I die,
> I want to die "easy" when I die,
> Shout "salvation" as I fly;
> I want to die "easy" when I die.

The repetitive line in this spiritual expresses an answer to the ultimate question raised a long time ago by the afflicted Job: "If a man die, shall he live again?" (Job 14:14). Ernest Estell, claiming to know how to handle the business of dying, certainly would have assented to the use of the philosophy contained in this folk chant.

Obviously, what is actually expressed in the phrase is that

he is in a state of readiness, not a statement made after the event of death has taken place. For how does one report an occurrence that is unreportable? Estell was reporting a conviction rather than an accomplished fact.

Does one feel something slip away when he dies? Does he lose something? Is death sleep? Is it peace? Is some palpable undocking experienced? No one has ever returned from beyond the veiled curtain to report the nature of the experience.

Allowing the songmakers to continue to supply the words for Ernest Estell, and thanking God for the clarity that flows from their simplicity of spirit that birthed the spirituals, we sing on:

> I want to die "easy" when I die,
> Shout "salvation" as I fly!

This man knew something of "salvation." It was the theme of his sermons, the object of his homiletical striving, the target at which he leveled his gospel gun. To make salvation a viable option for any man was his whole basis for preaching. His goal was to inspire his listener to seek and obtain salvation. He preached for a verdict. He preached for the full surrender of man's stubborn "no" to Christ's "yes," sealed as it was, should the man yield, with the promise of His own assuring words "Come to me, all who labor and are heavy laden, and I will give you rest" (Matthew 11:28, RSV).

On November 16, 1964, Ernest Coble Estell accepted Christ's invitation to rest. Yet, it would be easier to visualize him as loudly shouting "salvation" as he flew! We could "dig" him better in that stance.

Vernon Johns

He was frontier and pioneer, a plowboy from Virginia. As Paul Bunyan bestrode the primeval forests, this new Bunyan, with cleft chin erect, stumped the human forests with rustic, gangling tread, pole-axing hypocrisy with an avalanche of furious, booming, drawling passion. Not ungrammatically, but always grandiloquently, he outraged the king's English with glass-shattering Vernonian assaults that could rival the utterances of Casey Stengel, the colorfully vocal baseball manager whose use of the language has become proverbial.

Vernon Johns, a mulatto, was not immediately recognizable as a soul brother. His closely cropped brownish-red hair, seldom covered, ran wire-straight — not kinky — from hairline to the nape of his neck, and the gray in it bore evidence of the years. The appearance of noticeably crossed eyes was slightly relieved by his glasses. His eyes, one slightly less shut than the other, impressed one as having an Oriental narrowness. Looking at him, one could be deceived into thinking that he was perpetually tired. But his movements, slow and plodding, were relentless. The pert bit of moss on his upper lip which passed for a moustache was perceptible only in profile, but it became conspicuous when he was on the verge of an anguish-laden retort or a devastating remark.

Vernon Johns — he had no middle initial — was born in 1892 in Farmville, Prince Edward County, Virginia. His parents were the Reverend and Mrs. Willie Johns. His father, a Baptist country preacher-farmer, certainly left his map to this son, for he obviously followed many of the marks thereon.

This author remembers Vernon's mother as a great, towering influence. She met me at the door upon my only visit to the farm. She had the impact of quiet force of wisdom and common sense. She was a woman of Calpurnian grandeur who evidently had an all-pervasive pride in the possession and love of life. Her admiration for the great son she had brought forth was matched by her understandable anxiety for his fate as he fought for the rights of his brothers, situated as he was in an inimicable environment, not a prudent one for involvement in racial matters. She did not embrace the dangerous unorthodoxies of her son with dumb resignation; but, sensing his partnership with God, she offered him as a catalyst who might bring deliverance to less-endowed, fearful souls.

Altona Trent Johns was Vernon's brilliant wife, the daughter of a college president. She was the quintessence of scholarly flawlessness, charm, and ideal rearing. The author will ever be grateful for the kind fates that brought him into fellowship with her as he substituted for the organist on a warm, August night in his father's church in New Rochelle. As he played a selection by Chaminade under the duress of the demands of the occasion, Altona, an accomplished musician, followed with a trained ear, and they were tied in a musical thralldom. Glowing in the wake of her praise, he felt the beginning of a friendship which has remained through the years. Not only was she a musician, but she was the author of books on the subject of play songs and other helps for children. Her abilities and graces made her husband what he could not have been without her.

Altona bore a constellation of Vernon's children in what may be called a hexagonal pattern of two threes. First, there were three boys, "there, there, and there." Then there followed three girls. The eldest, Increase, named for his father's favorite professor, Edward Increase Bosworth, betrayed his father's proclivity for things rural by giving his cow the unlikely name "Bunghole." Said his proud father, "Can't nobody milk that cow but Increase."

The fact that the other two boys were as vivid as Increase with his cow is attested by the following incident. Vernon Johns, who respected the experience of the author's mother, took the train to New Rochelle to seek her advice. "Sister Boddie," he said, "give me some pearls of wisdom that will assist me in the successful bringing up of my three boys." Flattered, she spent the afternoon in giving from her treasured store. He thanked her and left. A month later, Johns still had the same agony, same dilemma; but now he had found success. Again he traveled to New Rochelle. This time he said, "Sister Boddie, I have discovered the best pedagogy that can be used in the most effective handling of my boys." Sweetly and expectantly, Mother asked, "What is it, Dr. Johns?"

"KILL 'EM!" he roared.

It is probable that the arrival of three daughters calmed him down sufficiently to temper the entire familial assemblage.

A BRAIN OF A MAN

With red, Virginia clay upon his shoes, the plowboy appeared at Oberlin College as out of the blue and announced to the dean: "I want to enroll at your school." The dean's reluctant assent, given against what he considered his better judgment, was vindicated when the college helped to produce one of the nation's greatest astonishments.

Some know a little about everything, others much about a few things; but Vernon Johns knew a great deal about many things. Moreover, the authoritative and engaging way he had of pouring out his sluices of erudition was more staggering than the fact that he possessed so much. His mastery of language, use of imagery, and the breathtaking wizardry of his descriptions are characteristics which ever hold him in the memory of those who heard him, even when he was at his worst. Like Amos renouncing the lazy "kine of Bashan," like Paul lowering the boom on the prejudiced coterie gathered around Mars' Hill, Vernon

Johns excoriated, needled, cajoled, angered, rebuked, and thoroughly shook up his listeners. On not a few occasions, his use of grammar was noticeable more in the breach than in the observance of technically correct rules; yet, his often brash, coarse, and abrasive speech made it clear that he would not tolerate the fracturing of truth or beauty made to bleed.

Early, this brain of a man bathed himself in books and set his scholastic sights high. With the certitude of Lincoln vowing to abolish slavery, he set out to raise the aspirations and hopes of his race to high levels of achievement, using his beloved farm as the cadre to set the example and to live out his principles. He was able to crash many an intellectual circle as a speaker by his easy and frequent references to the likes of Thomas Carlyle, Edna St. Vincent Millay, and G. A. Studdert-Kennedy, as well as lesser lights. Although white listeners from the Old Dominion were in no mood to accept the notion that a brash young black man could attain such high scholarship, Johns's honors won at college and seminary destroyed any such myth. Once Oberlin Professor Edward Increase Bosworth was asked by a colleague, "Who is your most promising student?" He replied, "You don't know him; he's a Negro named Vernon Johns — the only student who ever frightened me out of my boots when, in class, he raised a questioning hand, because I doubted my ability to answer correctly."

Johns read with an insatiable greed and hunger. Once, in one of his reading hideaways, he was so absorbed in a book that he failed to notice that his neglected meal was being shared by a rodent!

He moved with familiar intimacy among scholars, philosophers, poets, and social theorists, both well-known and obscure. He excelled in historical reference and grasped with mercurial facility the profoundest ideas of the most obscure scholars in whatever discipline was being propounded. No tome, however formidable, was inscrutable to him. His own intuitive depth of knowledge would easily have made it possible for him to have projected a set of norms as innovative and creative as those offered by people who were highly skilled in their own fields. His professors themselves sat at his feet and took notes during his recitations, often reversing the roles of Saul and Gamaliel.

Actually, he had the ability to set up his own curriculum and to construct his own agenda.

His sermon preached in the chapel at Colgate Rochester Divinity School was typical of the mark he was to make. Speaking on the subject "Tumultuous Preachers," the letter and spirit of the address were perfectly expressed in the text: "These that have turned the world upside down are come hither also" (Acts 17:6b). One such was he.

A tragic fire may, in part, explain his obscurity, especially among white scholars, though he was a legend among his racial peers. In the fire, a complete manuscript of a book entitled *Human Possibilities* was destroyed. According to Dr. Samuel L. Gandy, he had produced also another manuscript, *Immorality*, which in all likelihood was consumed by the same flames. Much more may have been lost; a few of his writings are left, however, and for this we must be thankful. In reporting the event which brought about his losses, he wrote: "A purifying fire came through here the other day and burnt up everything from the grand piano to the baby's pot." Such lightheartedness convinces one that he always remained above, and not under, his circumstances.

INCONGRUITIES

Vernon Johns was a kaleidoscope of abilities, moods, and surprises. So sweeping in scope were his ideological pronouncements, so ponderous, staggering, and grandiose were they, that in very few respects was he as big as his point of view. He could not abide a climate that thrived upon nostalgia, nostrums, shibboleths, platitudes, and clichés. He was not one to shrink from taking the plunge into ideas that were weighty, but always he projected too far, too impatiently, and too graspingly.

Once he bellowed, "You say you want a definition of perpetual motion?" Boiling up a storm of frowning blackness, he growled, "Give the average Negro a Cadillac and tell him to park it on some land that he owns."

His own car was no Cadillac. Called "The Creeping Thing," its name was in keeping with its looks, but not its speed. A wild ride in the ancient vehicle convinced one that the man and the "thing" assuredly went along together.

Riding a slow train through Arkansas, he welcomed a lengthy stop for refreshments. "Come here, boy," he called. But another voice brought the vendor about, veering him away from Dr. Johns. "COME HERE, BOY," roared Johns, to the consternation of the Caucasian interloper. The boy, frightened nearly out of his wits by such a bellow, resumed his approach to Johns. The other man, smarting from the sting of being jilted by one of his very own ethnic kin, came toward Johns menacingly, scornfully, and bellicose bent, only to be brought to a sudden halt by a stern warning that was backed by no mean guarantee: "Just crease your lips, and your brains will be mingled with the gravel!" But a horrifying sequel must be told.

Back in Montgomery, absentminded as ever, Johns drove through a red light and was apprehended. And who was sitting on the judge's bench hearing traffic violations that day but the man whose brains were almost mingled with the gravel! Revolting incongruities like this kept his effectiveness at a minimum in the city where another great man broke a bus business. Johns was known in infamy, not in endearment. If he were a saint, it was in Caesar's household, not in whitey's.

Two episodes reveal the peculiar earthiness of this denizen of the sod. Once he was introduced by the author's morally straitlaced father as a scholar-preacher who shunned tobacco. After many more glowing words of praise, Johns finally arose to speak. Smarting under so benign a tribute, he pulled out a handkerchief — and with it, three cigars, which dropped to the pulpit floor! They settled at the feet of the pious parson like three accusing fingers!

On another occasion Johns had accepted an invitation to speak in company with a quartet of singers from the seminary. Subsequently, he inadvertently accepted another appointment on the same date. Attempting to avoid a catastrophe in public relations, one of the young singers asked him, "What shall we do to avoid a conflict in dates?" For his well-meant concern, he received the bellowing rejoinder, "We'll cross that bridge when we come to it!"

On one of the author's frequent visits to preach in his brother's church in Baltimore, Johns arrived early enough to say surreptitiously, "Tim doesn't know it, but I've got fifty hams stashed away in the baptismal candidates' dressing room. I'm featuring them." But the heat of the July afternoon brought on such an olfactory impression that his announcement was superfluous. Tim, and everyone else, knew that almost literally "there was something rotten" in the cellar.

The author's own personal experience as the youthful co-proprietor of one of Johns's retail outlets revealed serious business incongruity. Soon after opening, The Boddie Brothers Fruit and Vegetable Market, on Horton Avenue, New Rochelle, was forced by weird circumstances to seek other than the originally intended source of supply. In fact, on opening day itself, no promised produce was forthcoming. When a tardy shipment finally arrived from Long Island, the merchandise was tired and unattractive. Vegetables which should have been green were haggard and brown. Others were green where they should have been brown. Hams, hazardously ashen, defied all house-wifely skills to desalinize them. In a word, Johns's farm products were a catastrophe.

No more successful was his book-selling enterprise involving cross-country contacts. His worthy motive, aimed at the enlightenment of his brethren, was blunted for the want of so much as a dram of that indispensable expertise which eluded him. He never seemed to learn how to make money. His economics did not match his grand point of view.

Johns had a lofty ideal regarding work. Sartorially, Sunday made a difference; vocationally, sabbath had no end. He equated religion with work. The Master was a carpenter, "a worker." Labor Day to him was no mere chronological reflex, but was one of the calendar's shining days. His philosophy of work was so assiduously engaged in and faithfully carried out in his life that he was the source of embarrassment to the members of his Charleston, West Virginia, parish. Despite his custom of not wearing a hat, a head covering would appear when he was acting as a farmer selling his products. The potato vendor, ill-befitting his role as scholar and pulpiteer, wore an old, beaten-up cap which, as though he were some old Dobbin, gave him surcease from heat-borne torment. One day a deacon waited upon him to discuss whether or not he was allowing his farm to get between him and his church. He replied, "Oh, I was afraid you came to remind me that I was allowing my church to get between me and my farm!"

It was the passion of Johns to convert his listeners to the conviction that God was best praised and worshiped, not with loud amens and hosannas, but by hard, hand-wrung, grubbing production. Happy is the man who toils in the fields and is enriched by his efforts thereby! If, under religious auspices, however spurious they may have been regarded, Father Divine could build one of the most effective consumer cooperatives, then Johns could at least attempt to rear a rural monument to God's glory by exalting the healthy, soiled, calloused, work-worn, black hand raised heavenward in thankful praise for work to do and strength to do it.

His attempts, noble but abortive, failed largely because of his love for the farm. He overlooked the black migration from agrarian to urban centers. Were his attention but centered upon more sophisticated avenues of work, such as sales, business, and other white- and blue-collar, cash-yielding enterprises, more people might have paid attention to his expounding of economic theories. Too few could understand the strange alliance between the preaching of the Word of God and the "derogatory" tilling of the recalcitrant sod. But he lacked the time, stamina, or know-how to comprehend opportunities for alternate kinds of service. Thus, his appeal was limited to only the faithful few, because it seemed that he himself was a failure as a producer. He had the idiosyncrasy of having no carry-over from his philosophy to his realistic, factual situation. He was done in by the existential.

SQUARE-JAWED PROPHET

Vernon Johns needled the power structure unmercifully. His sermon "God and Carter Glass" exposed the Old Dominion's casuistries and hypocrisies. The take-off of a then current book, *The Vanishing Virginian*, suggesting that some obituaries should be listed in the newspapers' public improvements columns, raised both eyebrows and temperatures when the following sermon title was advertised in the paper: "Some Virginians that Ought to Vanish." A committee of upset community fathers called upon him and asked why he had advertised so pointedly.

Acidly they were told, "It must have proven effective: you are here."

As a preacher, no living person seemed to be able to "flesh out" the homiletical bones with such skill and originality and to throw kisses at the Pleiades with such astounding aplomb and deftness. His sermonic cadences seemed almost as though they were set to music, and the bodily surges associated with his delivery would induce audience sympathetic vibration worthy of a Howard Thurman.

His vocabulary flowed from eternal springs. He never had to work at it; he came preaching. His voice thundered forth with conviction, authority, and erudition. To try accurately to describe his forensic power would preempt all adjectives. He was a creator in the realm of "imagineering"; a satirist whose subtle and strident humor tempered the merciless barb of rebuke, he knew how to soften his polemics precisely to the point of toleration, if not acceptance, by the sheer power of his expressive genius. While killing his audience, he was thrilling it.

The listener supplied the humor, while the speaker, deadly serious in his ponderous and poignant rebuke, loudly poured it on. As he forged ahead, one could feel the powerful surge of passion oozing from his every pore as the six-feet bulk of roaring exhortation, stoked by the terrible need felt by this square-jawed prophet to shake his race loose from the indolence and lethargy that strangled it, lashed out with withering tongue to correct the condition. Brain power, lung power, and body power were all there. At home on campus or farm, pulpit or dais, cloister or mart, he was poet, seer, mystic, sage, and saint. He inspired students, unstuffed stuffed shirts, tweaked aristocratic noses, and punctured captiousness, infuriating, spellbinding, overpowering, and making use of every weapon in his God-supplied arsenal. The man was the epitome of sheer brilliance, grandiloquence, and perspicacity.

He shook with his abrasive manner, not because of any native brutality or harshness, but because of his possession of an unbridled, restless passion which led him to declare eternal warfare upon the tyranny of oppression which had held his people in shameful bondage for so long. His protests belied a logic which in all likelihood he revered in his calmer moments. But the plight of his people reduced him to a pettiness which defied reason. Stupidities which even a child would scorn were brought forth by his impatience when he was in the blue mood invoked by memories of the exploitation that dehumanized his brothers.

As John the Baptist was "the voice of one crying in the wilderness, Make straight the way of the Lord," Vernon Johns fallowed the ground which provided the seedbed for the germination of the great movement led by another, whose name was Martin Luther King, Jr. The Dexter Avenue Baptist Church, worship center for the cream of Montgomery's black bourgeoisie, called Johns as pastor before the coming of Dr. King. The martyred leader's ministry was found acceptable largely because Vernon Johns had already passed that way.

Of course, the civil rights movement reached its zenith in the work of King. However, the movement was started by Johns, pastor of the Dexter Avenue Baptist Church, from whose crucible Montgomery, Alabama's first dramatic encounter was poured. According to Altona Johns, Bob Smith of the *Charlotte News* told her that "Vernon was the prime mover of civil rights in Prince Edward County." Any veteran citizen of Montgomery will attest to who started the "ruction."

During the school tug-of-war in Prince Edward County, an acquaintance chided Johns for not being in on the movement, and drew this drawling rebuttal, "Well, no, I really didn't do anything, but my niece was the person who instituted the first suit to integrate the schools there." Bob Smith's book *They Closed the Schools* depicts the heroic role of Vernon Johns as he quarterbacked the rebellion.

The theological basis for Johns's crusade is disclosed in this direct quote from one of his sermons:

> The nastiest and deadliest problem before the world today is the insane hatred between races. Life is bearable because of the variety it offers, yet here are men hating other men to the murder point, legislating against children before they are born because their skins, circumstances and background are different. If one opens his mind on the subject of religion, he may have to keep it open on the subject of justice.

If power had color for Johns, it was green (the color of money); but he did not envision any Marshall Plan type of financing to sustain welfare programs for the poor and the black people. It is unlikely that he would have thought up the reparations idea to mollify the grievances of slavery days. His thoughts lacked the latitude of contemporary malcontents. He shaped the philosophy of King, not the economics. Johns provided the rationale for the movement; King dramatized it.

Great educators, such as Benjamin Mays, and sterling professors, such as George Kelsey, Howard Thurman, Sam Williams, and Lucius Tobin, set the direction and reared a skeleton. Vernon Johns sparked the incentive that fleshed out the bones into a strong body, which became The Movement under Martin Luther King, Jr. After Montgomery came Albany; after that came the road to destiny, fame, and crucifixion at Memphis. The important area where indeed Johns was bigger than his point of view is that in which he declared war to the death upon the injustice suffered by his people.

He often stressed the point that in some situations in the South, the Negro had to either swallow his pride or "lose his hide." Johns himself never did either. Lacking the graces, if not the charisma, of his successor at Dexter Avenue, he cared less, if at all, for the white man's affection. Seeing love as a privilege rather than a right, he accepted it only after justice was first bestowed. He demanded justice above all else.

Dr. Samuel L. Gandy, dean of the School of Religion, Howard University, writes these stirring words about Vernon Johns:

> Each man who sincerely seeks to live authentically desires in all earnestness to be worthy of his time and generation. To be worthy may simply mean to be acceptable: observing the conventionalities, honoring the polite occasions, acknowledging the rank and status symbols, conforming to the cultural patterns uncritically, reiterating familiar phrases, ritualistically. To be a man, that is a person, in one's time and generation, may require more: courage and prophetic spirit. Vernon Johns, great American preacher, a rugged individualist, was a man.

There is no more lofty accolade.

Johns's vivid word pictures, so striking as to take away one's breath, find expression in sentences such as this from a speech delivered on Hitler's fiftieth birthday: "The only problem that was Adolf Hitler's forty-nine years ago along about now was how to get his big toe into his mouth."

Armed with the text "If the borders of Ephraim be too small

for thee, go to the woods and cut down the trees," he flung down the gauntlet to the provincial, timid, habit-doped mortal, "knee bent and body bowed" not in prayer but despondency.

His abrasiveness is revealed in the following vignette. Over the remains of an unfortunate Charlestonian who died in a brawl, came forth these exact, incredible, and only words: "Anyone who stops by a grog shop with his paycheck instead of going straight home to his wife and family with it ought to be struck over the head with a ball bat and killed. The benediction will take place at the cemetery."

One can see why the Reverend J. Raymond Henderson suggested that Vernon Johns be endowed to do nothing but traverse the country irritating the Negro. Although he berated him, Johns loved his soul brother. He excoriated him in a sermon "What Is the Number?" It was a brutal satire on the pinch-penny gambling game that was so popular with the deprived and ghetto-spawned black. He did it because he loved him. ("Whom the Lord loveth he chasteneth.") No vice, no short-coming that thwarted black economic progress escaped his rapier thrust. His admiration was great for those of other ethnic groups whose organizational genius guaranteed their cohesion and mutual strength. He used their frugality and monetary responsibility to shame the Negro, with his painful antics, into like behavior.

The shafts which he sank into the soft underbelly of chauvinism and imperialistic nationalism were sharp, repetitive, and cruel. His sermon "God and England," a case in point, stands as one of the most condemning of its kind. Listen:

So far flung is the British domain that she can boast that upon her remotest shore the sun never sets. But can this be because in the bosom of many of her subjects the sun never rises?

Rudyard Kipling came in for censure for writing in his "Recessional":

> If, drunk with sight of power, we loose
>   Wild tongues that hold not Thee in awe,
> Such boasting as the Gentiles use,
>   Or lesser breeds without the Law—
> Lord God of Hosts, be with us yet,
>   Lest we forget—lest we forget!

His quarrel is not with the poetry, but with the exclusiveness, the pattern of divisiveness, all so foreign to the way of the Master. In another verse of it:

> Far-called, our navies melt away;
>   On dune and headland sinks the fire:
> Lo, all our pomp of yesterday
>   Is one with Nineveh and Tyre!
> Judge of the Nations, spare us yet,
>   Lest we forget—lest we forget!

Vernon Johns could not overlook the apartheid expressed in "lesser breeds without the Law" — aloof, mean, impersonal — which made the Empire "one with Nineveh and Tyre." His pulpit was the floor of Parliament, the Forum of Rome, the Congress of the United States. With universal and prophetic tongue he denounced the crimes of national ambition and the wounds inflicted upon the human family. Anything that smacked of human oppression or carried the slightest tinge or vestige of hated slavery turned him into a raging lion out of its cage.

Shakespeare wrote of "sermons in stones, and good in everything." The bard of Avon should have lived to hear the sermon called "Epitaphs" by Vernon Johns, delivered on the occasion of the opening of a new funeral parlor. Here are some of the gems in stone:

> A. Life is a jest and all things show it;
>   I thought so once, and now I know it.[1]

> B. A shipwrecked sailor buried on this coast
>   Bids you set sail;
>   Full many a gallant barque when we were lost
>   Weathered the gale.[2]

> C. This be the verse you grave for me:
>   *Here he lies where he longed to be;*
>   *Home is the sailor, home from the sea,*
>   *And the hunter home from the hill.*[3]

Whatever was achieved for that mortuary accrued for the living dead who heard that sermon and were born again on that July afternoon.

[1] John Gay
[2] Anonymous
[3] Robert Louis Stevenson, "Requiem" in *Great Poems of the English Language* (New York: Tudor Publishing Co., 1927), p. 1093.

Johns was extremely impatient with ignorance on parade. At a conference, a man who wanted to become a bishop came to Henry Hitt Crane and said: "There seems to be a conspiracy of silence against my becoming bishop. What do you advise?" Crane replied: "If I were you, I'd join the conspiracy." This story characterizes the spirit of Vernon Johns. As a gentleman of limited gray matter was hogging the floor at an association meeting, Johns cried, "IT BEHOOVES HIM TO SIT DOWN AND BE QUIET!"

A provocative sermon, "Rock Foundations," reflected his rugged faith. The text was Matthew 7:24-25. He said:

Time works havoc with our most treasured possessions. Beauty turns to ashes beneath its touch. The channels of rivers and the course of history change. Debris piles on the face of queens and kings, and seashells are left stranded on mountain tops. Our health, our wealth, our friends, our ascendency go whirling away in the current of the years. When the sands have run sufficiently, they leave Nineveh but a name and the Parthenon a heap of rubbish. . . . "But whoever hears these words of mine," says Jesus, "and doeth them, shall be likened unto a wise man who built his house upon a rock."

An excerpt from one of his writings sets a contemporary controversy, gun-control legislation, into sermonic perspective:

I have an acquaintance, a practical man, who is alarmed that I travel without a pistol. "I need one," says he, "to fight off robbers. . . ." Thus far I have not encountered the robbers. When I do and the robbers go off with my money, I want them to leave me intact. Staging a pistol duel with a gunman, with my pocket change as the stake, strikes me as nonsense. . . . My honor? I can find better ways to be honorable. My courage? Courage is not properly measured by notches on the butts of our guns.

Vernon Johns's sermon "Transfigured Moments" was published in a homiletical journal. Accompanying the sermon was the editor's preface, later published also in *Best Sermons, 1926.* The complimentary remarks were:

Mr. Johns is the first colored preacher to appear in *Best Sermons,* and it is both an honor and a joy to bid him welcome, alike for his race and his genius. . . .

Aside from his labor as a minister of a great church, Mr. Johns finds time to preach and lecture in many colleges and at various religious and educational conferences. . . . The sermon lifts us into a higher air, above the fogs of passion and prejudice, where the ages answer, antiphonally, telling us of the brotherhood of man in the life of God in Christ.[4]

When Vernon Johns recommended the author to the pulpit committee for the pastorate of the First Baptist Church of Huntington, West Virginia, he said, "He's my kind of preacher! Get him!"

THE ROMANCE OF DEATH

Only ten days before his own passing, Johns preached a sermon entitled "The Romance of Death." His wife was to write:

> Always, I suppose, I will be immobilized by the shock, especially since Vernon had his heart attack two days before he was to leave the hospital where he had what was termed a "successful operation."

Vernon Johns never crashed the headlines. He failed to attain the renown of his great civil rights pupil. Was the time not ripe for Vernon Johns? The arrival of Martin Luther King, Jr., on the public scene coincided with the onslaught of the full impact of the 1954 Supreme Court decision on school desegregation. But Vernon Johns did not ride the crest of any such wave. The sad truth is that his obscurity in the consciousness of white America was the result of the hideous legacy of segregation and discrimination.

The great humanitarian Johann Friedrich Oberlin never visited the United States. However, the well-known American institution, Oberlin College, at Oberlin, Ohio, bears his name. One of its sons, Vernon Johns, after almost being refused admission by the administration, was joyfully acknowledged by that same administration as the embodiment of the spirit and a vindication of the faith of Oberlin himself.

This plowboy from Virginia paved the way for other eager blacks. He brought honor and glory to other prisoners of hope whose achievements and resourcefulness established Oberlin College as a school of the prophets. From the lowly performance of farm chores to the heady business of shepherding aristocratic churches, Vernon Johns never lost his common touch, his salty humor, nor his impossible dream.

[4] Joseph Fort Newton, ed., *Best Sermons, 1926* (New York: Harcourt Brace Jovanovich, Inc., 1925-1926), p. 332.

Martin Luther King, Jr.

The confident baritone voice repeatedly proclaimed, "I have a dream," as a crowd of two hundred thousand souls listened. Before he began, John Lewis, Walter Reuther, and Roy Wilkins had made speeches. Marian Anderson sang, then the main speaker was introduced, whereupon the applause became as thunder and the band played "The Battle Hymn of the Republic." Who was the dreamer? He was Martin Luther King, Jr.

He was an authentic scholar, human and humane, and a man of the people — a man for all seasons. His life's thrust was made through the medium of preaching. If this had not been the case, his hearers might have stopped their ears and his detractors torn him to pieces. His cool head exalted him, but his warm heart saved him. King does not appear in these pages because of his prodigious accomplishments on behalf of civil rights, although his ideals cannot be completely separated from his homiletical prowess. Others have written of his achievements with adulation and exaltation more cogently, to the point of almost exhausting the supply of material. He is included in these pages because he meets the same criteria as those set for others in this study, and only for that reason. He is remembered here because he was a black Baptist, intellectual, and physically alive preacher. Because of this, his niche is assured.

CREATED EQUAL

Martin Luther King, Jr., was born on January 15, 1929, at the end of the Roaring Twenties, just as the last tint of pre-depression glow was wearing off. As Pippa passed, all was just about to become quite wrong with the world. His father was Martin Luther King, a well-known Baptist minister, and his mother was the daughter of the Reverend Alfred Daniel Williams, founder of the Ebenezer Baptist Church, Atlanta, Georgia. Both Martin and his father were really named "Michael," and during his boyhood and youth he was called "Mike"; but there came a moment when the father assumed the historic "Martin Luther" for both himself and his son. Was this son's new name a portent that he would spark a new reformation of the church?

At first he was undecided as to what direction he would take in his studies, but he finally yielded to the call to become a Baptist minister. Already, at Washington High School, he had been awarded the Elks' oratorical prize. He graduated from Morehouse College in June, 1948, having won the Webb Oratorical Contest in his senior year. From there, he entered the Crozer Theological Seminary, in Chester, Pennsylvania, where he became well acquainted with Dr. J. Pius Barbour. Respected by his fellows, he was made president of the student body. Upon his graduation in June, 1951, he was the valedictorian, received the Pearl M. Plafker Citation for the most outstanding student, and won the J. Lewis Crozer Fellowship for graduate study. In September he entered Boston University as a doctoral candidate in philosophy, taking some of his graduate courses at Harvard. Before he was through all of his education, he had examined the thinking of such giants as Hegel, Thoreau, Gandhi, Harnack, and Emerson; and he had sat at the feet of Howard Thurman, Sam Williams, George Kelsey, and Lucius Tobin.

During his years of graduate study, on June 18, 1953, he married Coretta Scott, a promising singer. Eventually, the couple became blessed with four children, Martin Luther III, Dexter Scott, Yolande Denise, and Bernice Albertine.

Martin Luther King saw justice for all races, especially his own, for whom it had been an illusion for too long a time, as his all-consuming passion. The challenge would not down. Therefore, pursuing his objective as though he were relentlessly hunting the Holy Grail itself, he set off, as it were, upon his charger until the unrelenting surge of that white steed carried him into Valhalla. Borne upon the tremendous brain of Vernon Johns and the sore feet of Rosa Parks, not to mention the lift he received from his parsonage rearing, he invaded the fray for racial justice which took thirteen years of striving, from Montgomery to Memphis. Vernon Johns paved the way as pastor-predecessor at the Dexter Avenue Baptist Church of Montgomery, Alabama. The weary woman on the now famous, but then obscure, bus did the rest. The confluence of these two mighty streams provided the rushing current that carried him to notoriety, adulation, fame, and death.

In the nineteen twenties the important piece of legislation touching human rights had been the Dyer Bill to outlaw the foul practice of lynching. Inasmuch as the black man was chiefly involved, Congress moved at an unusually plodding pace. After a long time, it gave the bill an affirmative clearance. There remained to be dealt with, however, a dubious bit of nonsense described as "separate but equal." Segregation remained an impregnable legislative Berlin Wall, as rock-ribbed as Gibraltar, throughout the youth and early adulthood of Martin. The legal aspect of segregation crumbled with the rendering of the famous Supreme Court Decision of 1954 outlawing segregation in the public schools of the land, but the practice of segregation did not come to an end.

DREAMER

He was invited to become a candidate for the pulpit of the Dexter Avenue Baptist Church. With some trepidation, he applied his philosophic mind to a consideration of the human being. As a result, he brought with him his sermon entitled "The Three Dimensions of a Complete Life," which he had polished to near perfection. The sermon was received so enthusiastically that there was no doubt about his being called to be the pastor of the church. He was to use the same thoughts in future appearances in pulpits.

One of his sermons bears the title "A Cool Head and a Warm Heart." The text was "Be ye therefore wise as serpents, and harmless as doves" (Matthew 10:16b). The idea epitomized his very nature. He was a man with a baptized brain and a heart of compassion, both in happy balance. As clean a writer as his day has produced, he could have earned his living at writing. His metaphysical mind loved Hegelian dialectic, and the homely philosopher's epistemology wove itself through his sermonic discourses. "Thesis becomes antithesis, which, in turn, becomes synthesis," he would drone, spinning out dialectical yarn upon the homiletical wadmal of perpetual weaving and passing of the shuttle of incomprehensible expression back and forth upon itself in weary cadence and continuous self-perpetuating movement *ad infinitum.*

Notwithstanding, Martin knew how to turn such complications into simplicity while he preached the virtues of love, forgiveness, and redemption. As a preacher, he was as wise as the serpent and harmless as the dove; he had a cool head but a warm heart.

He readily sermonized at the drop of a hint. When he was asked to lecture on the subject "How to Organize a Boycott," he brought forth "Paul's Letter to the American Churches," probably as powerful an utterance as has been heard in this century. Also, his "Letter from Birmingham Jail" is a sermon. Martin felt a close affinity with the apostle Paul, who wrote to the churches in the Graeco-Roman world. Accordingly, Martin Luther King, Jr., wielded his provocative pen to chastise the bewildered churches in the American culture.

He openly despised the indifference and inertia that existed in the ranks of "The Great Unconcerned." His barbs at the good but silent white folks were stinging in their rebuke. Whenever he castigated those who were so afflicted, he always did it with the touch of the Master's concern, interpreting such sloth as the enemy of their own well-being and the destroyer of their very souls. All this he did deftly by using the format of the preaching Word.

Perhaps King is most widely remembered for his part in the

March on Washington, on August 28, 1963. The nation was mindful of the hundredth anniversary of the signing of the Emancipation Proclamation by Abraham Lincoln. With the March on Washington, the cloud that seemed to be only the size of a man's hand on the horizon became a wild, threatening storm to all enemies of freedom. King was chosen to be the principal, and final, speaker of the day. After a long parade of the nation's best entertainment talent and another long sequence of addresses by prominent persons, his assignment to speak to a quarter of a million tired, sweltering people was not an enviable one. But King did what none would have believed was possible: he held the crowd in his hand.

Beginning with a reference to the emancipator of a hundred years before, he proclaimed that the Negro was still not free. Calling upon the Declaration of Independence, he pointed out that all men are created equal. Then he spoke of his dream; it was a dream that his four little children would some day be treated not on the basis of the color of their skin, but rather on the quality of their characters. Further, he had a dream that "Every valley shall be exalted, and every mountain and hill shall be made low: and the crooked shall be made straight" (Isaiah 40:4). After the use of spiritual and Scripture, he told that his dream was that all, without exception, would be able to sing "My country, 'tis of Thee . . . From every mountain side let freedom ring!" Finally, his audience was electrified as he continued to tell of his dream. He looked forward to the day when freedom would ring from every village and hamlet across the nation and all men would be able to join in singing that old Negro spiritual, "Free at last! Free at last! Thank God almighty, we are free at last!"

In mid May, 1964, he made his way to the sessions of the American Baptist Convention in Atlantic City, New Jersey. Here he received the Dahlberg Peace Award, and his acceptance speech, which was in truth a sermon, shook the very foundations of the auditorium, and all but emptied the halls of other Baptist bodies that were meeting simultaneously under the one giant roof.

Six passengers were sharing the taxi that was to run from the Philadelphia airport to Atlantic City. There was a delay of fifteen minutes before Dr. King arrived, and some of the passengers began to chafe with impatience. But as soon as they discovered the identity of the distinguished passenger for whom they were waiting, their impatience turned into a sense of wonder at the presence of a dangerous greatness. A timid, white sailor offered the plain back of his ticket envelope for a precious signature, which was gladly proffered. Emboldened by this act, all the rest of the riders requested and received his autograph. Without a doubt, Martin Luther King, Jr., was the greatest Christian to walk on the famous Atlantic City boardwalk during that Convention.

None could scorn him for being ignorant, especially after he was chosen to receive the Nobel Prize for Peace. Standing at the rostrum in the Oslo University Auditorium on Thursday, December 10, 1964, he spoke of the long struggle of the American Negro for racial justice and anticipated the time when all would recognize that they enjoyed a more noble civilization because of the suffering of those who struggled.

To be sure, there were those who were jealous of his prestige and who spread false tales about him but, like his Lord who was called Beelzebub, he carried this extra burden as the great soldier of the cross that he truly was. He had overcome.

FREE AT LAST

When King was needed in Memphis, he came in a dark mood. For a month, he had not been himself. On Wednesday evening, April 3, 1968, there was a mass meeting at Mason Temple. The weather being inclement, King decided not to go, and he asked Ralph Abernathy to preside over the meeting. In spite of the bad weather, the temple was filled to overflowing. Abernathy telephoned King at the motel and told him that the place was packed and the people were anxious to hear him. In the middle of the evening, and with no immediate preparation for the speech he was to make, King responded to the call and entered the hall.

On the platform, King revealed his premonition that he might be near the end of his life. He told of attempts and threats against his life made by blacks as well as by whites. Going on, he said:

Well, I don't know what will happen now. But it really doesn't matter with me now. . . . I just want to do God's will. And he's allowed me to go up to the mountain. And I've looked over, and I've seen the promised land.

Less than twenty-four hours later, as he stood on the balcony outside his motel room, a single shot brought him down. For him, the promised land had become a reality.

From April 4 through and a bit beyond April 9, 1968, the world was bathed in a sweeping tide of deep, melancholy reverence. It was an eerie, strange kind of reverence. It was all the more profound because Easter was only a half dozen days away. The sight of the mule-drawn farm wagon, bearing the coffin of the fallen prophet, exhibited on the television screens of millions, will not soon be forgotten. What had not yet been achieved in life had now been accomplished in death. The martyrdom in Memphis, as martyrdom always does, enshrined King for all time in eternal memory.

The New York Times revealed an appreciation for his preaching achievements when, on April 7, 1968, it published the following editorial feature:

Martin Luther King was a preacher, a man from Georgia and a Negro who became a golden-tongued orator, a spokesman for the Deep South and the Ghetto North, a symbol above color of undying yearnings and imperishable rights. He was an American in the truest historic sense: for he had a dream.

It seems to be worthy of notice that this editorial's first word of description of the man is "preacher."

Save for the officiating brothers, the absence of an appreciable number of Baptist clergymen from the funeral provides the cause for some bafflement. Perhaps the observations of Dean William C. Hull of the Southern Baptist Theological Seminary will help us to uncover some clue to the answer. He pointed out that although many might have debated the appropriateness of the philosophy, strategy, and methods of King, the underlying question which must be faced was "What was God trying to tell us through the ministry of the martyred prophet?" Hull went on to draw a parallel between King and his namesake, Martin Luther. He related the profound and long-lasting influence of the Reformation begun by Luther under the battle cry of "Justification by Faith." But, Hull recounted, as the years went by, the new life of the Reformation became calcified in systems of theology that shut out the relationship between men for the sake of emphasis upon the relationship of man with God. It was time for a new reformation. Martin Luther King, Jr., brought this new reformation with the watchword "Reconciliation by Love." Hull concluded by pointing up the desperate need for this word in the face of poverty, prejudice, and the threat of war.

King, the man who has caused the greatest astonishment of the era, is rightly extolled as a civil rights leader, a young and fearless prophet, a peacemaker of Nobel prizewinning proportions. Songs have been written and sung, raising his name in modern Ebenezers. After all, had he not brought the buses of cities to a screeching halt? Had he not rallied many to join him in sacrificing all for the sake of the dispossessed? Had he not attempted, on pain of blowing the whole civil rights concept sky high, to make the entire world peace conscious by making public his opposition to the war in Southeast Asia?

The London Observer, in the edition published on April 4, 1968, carried an article by Patrick O. Donovan entitled "A Terrible Death." We may do well to ponder some of the statements and attitudes in this article by Donovan. First, Donovan referred to King's rejection by his own people. Of Jesus, the Scripture says, "He came to his own home, and his own people received him not" (John 1:11, RSV). What was true for Jesus was certainly also true for Martin Luther King, Jr. With so many unlovely people inhabiting the earth, universal admiration for a man like him could not be expected. Further, numerous black people, while reckoning his ideals as noble and recognizing that he was a decent man, could not honestly share his faith nor embrace his point of view. Some rejected him on merely general principles. Some saw in him a threat to their own political power and prestige. Still others held the innate creaturely hate for him that they would hold for any man.

Difficult as it may be for Christians to conceive, there were enemies of Jesus whose only regret while he was hanging on the cross was that his sufferings were not more intense and the tenure of his agony no longer than three hours. So it was with

84

Martin. After all, it was one of his own race who made the first attempt upon his life.

Donovan referred to King's religion as the "opium of the blacks," a rather flippant Marxian gibe. If the eschatological reference is applied to King's religion, it should be universally applied. Is it not true that all religions relate to the hereafter in some way? If not, they cease to warrant being characterized as religion. Beyond this, in this dope-infested society called a social order it may be appropriate to devise the paraphrase:

> Religion is not the opium of the people, but
> Opium is the religion of the people.

Consider that couplet for a moment. A heroin-ingested dullness of conscience may have been a responsible contributory factor in the murder of Martin Luther King, Jr.

One final retort: Donovan commented that the laws did not change men's hearts; this may be factual and realistic. But men's hearts certainly could have been changed if there had been any enforcement of the laws.

TWO KENNEDYS AND A KING

In the quiet of White House calm, a meeting was underway. John Fitzgerald Kennedy was proving to be a most gracious host. He had rehearsed the recording of the nearly explosive, highly dramatic speech given at the Lincoln Memorial where the dream had been projected. As a consequence, the most meaningful of all civil rights legislative packages ever to be proposed came out of that historic meeting. With teeth-bearing urgency, it had been entered as a bill into the congressional hopper. If all that was contained in it were to be exalted into law, a crest of morale as high as that which accompanied the 1954 Supreme Court Decision would have borne up all of America's black citizenry.

A "do nothing" Congress, however, was looking the other way as proponents pled, argued, importuned, and prayed. But God was at work. His inscrutable wisdom called for the decisive and eventful journey of one who must needs go through Texas. This route turned out to be the Via Dolorosa for the youthful president, for in Dallas, Texas, he was shot and killed.

At the precise moment of his heartrending demise, life began for the dormant, nearly defunct civil rights package. In spite of the zestful enthusiasm of the murdered president, the civil rights legislation, for whatever sinister reason, was doomed to failure. His guidance would not have sufficed to steer the action successfully through those hostile congressional waters. As his optimism betrayed him in Texas, it would have proven just as treacherous in Washington had his life depended upon the promulgation of those proposals through the restive, suspicious, enigmatic body. But he was destined to be freed from such congressional embarrassment. Somewhat like Martin Luther King, Jr., John Fitzgerald Kennedy had been released from rejection by his own death.

If Senator Robert Kennedy had been able to purchase soul, he would have bought it by the ton. It was he who set out to pick up the tab for the Kennedy dynasty, which knew well the price of renown and fame. Belatedly, in the opinion of some, he set his sights upon the White House. After biding his time and ignoring the preeminence which the New Hampshire primary might have provided, he finally made his big move. In the glow of the eternal flame that had been lighted on November 25, 1963, he used his experience gained in the attorney general's role as a lever, as well as that of the office of membership in the world's most exclusive club, the United States Senate.

After a rocky start and near elimination, doubtless due to the procrastination which his friends feared, the sun finally burned through the clouds, as a victory in the California primary turned his fortunes around. But while he was thanking his supporters for their help in putting him across, an assassin from another clime waylaid him in the kitchen of a Los Angeles hotel and all but blew his head off at close range with a mean firearm. A day later, he joined his brother John. Another tragic, meaningless, infamous act gave to the nation a new trauma on a June day only a little less than three months after the death of Martin Luther King, Jr.

What did this bushy-haired Kennedy have to do with the prophet? The funeral service for King at the Ebenezer Baptist Church, Atlanta, may be recalled, when the crowd that had gathered outside had to be forced aside to make way for the arrival of the widow of the late president. Bobby was already inside, where he had been for hours. Very informally, he was occupying the pulpit area as though he owned it when the television cameras picked him up. Only after an usher signaled to him that the service was about to begin did he take his seat with other dignitaries on the front row. He had been politicking while waiting for the service to begin. His astute mind had an unfolding, aggressive plan.

Not only did he crave votes, but he felt the need of something more — vastly more. What he wished for was the power of a Martin Luther King, Jr., to face a gathering storm and be sustained through it, for he was sure it was brewing and being churned up especially for him. At the funeral service, when the tapes were playing the last sermon that came from Martin's lips, one wonders what Bobby's thoughts must have been when the voice proclaimed, "I've been to the mountaintop." Then the cry "Free at last!" burst upon his Roman Catholic ears uninitiated to the customary lung-propelled utterance of bombastic Baptist grandeur.

Here, at Ebenezer, lay one that had been struck down on the balcony outside a Memphis motel; Bobby was soon to be struck down in the murky kitchen of a Los Angeles hotel. The young black had just emerged from rest that was essential to sustain life when the bullet found him; Bobby was to fall in a life-ebbing heap in a place that produced the staff of life in its final edible form — bread for the body's sustenance. Sleep, bread, life — these three. Now only the wine of sacrifice was needed to sustain the lives of others; and that, too, was provided, symbolically, in the spilled blood of the two young dreamers, one who wanted to see his people overcome, and the other who thought it was not too late to build a better world. The sacrifices were executed by the hands of two deranged young men with trigger fingers too free to be permitted to function.

That the assassins were caught, tried, convicted, and sentenced is not important. That the three young men — two Kennedys and a King — set their faces steadfastly to go to their respective Jerusalems is important.

There is meaning in all of this for this author. It means that the power of the gospel has found its vindication in the constant drama of the tragedy of the unfulfilled becoming the glory of the unfulfilled. Just when we become qualified for a task, we have to lay it down. The preacher in this trinity would want to remind all who read his story that the gospel was the power that gave significance to his life and justified his existence. The gospel provided his reason for being, the rationale for all his endeavors.

If the ministry is to be upheld upon its lofty perch, men with the spirit of such "bad boys" as Martin Luther King, Jr., must be discovered, educated, and turned loose upon the evil forces of hate and destruction, As he cried, "Let the woman go free" when she stabbed him, he would have said the same about James Earl Ray.

That is the spirit of Christ.

CODA—Black Studies

The first Martin Luther King, Jr., Professor of Black Studies was installed at the Colgate Rochester/Bexley Hall/Crozer center for religious studies in Rochester, New York, on November 10, 1969. The investiture of Henry Haywood Mitchell was sealed by a charge and handclasps from President Gene Ebert Bartlett and Provost Milton Carl Froyd. Only a year before, Martin Luther King, Jr., had been remembered in a ceremony on the very same stage, as a black soprano movingly sang a number called "Dr. King." Now, at the installation, the choir sang "Nobody Knows the Trouble I've Seen," followed immediately by a choral rendition of a song written by Charles Walker, a brilliant young musician and preacher. This number was entitled "I've Been to the Mountain Top."

Then Dr. Mitchell gave his address of the evening, which he called "The Prophetic Dream and the Route Through Reality." The entire program reflected the panoramic sweep that gave rise to this history-making event. The stream of relevance had been set into motion by fourteen black students in the Divinity School who had raised two hundred and fifty thousand dollars — in addition to much noise and obstruction — to stimulate interest in the project.

By no stretch of the imagination could one have conceived the birth of such an academic thrust unless there had been a Martin Luther King, Jr. It was because of his life and work that both eyes and hearts were opened to the possibilities of this new type of enterprise, soon to become known throughout the land, we hope. Here was a tremendous resource for learning about black people in their happiest habitat, religion, at one of the nation's most significant seats of learning.

Professor Henry Mitchell is the author of two works whose titles speak eloquently. "The Dimensions of Demand" is the title of an article of his that appeared in *The Crusader;* "A Report on the Dream" is the title of a brochure. For our purposes, the contents of the brochure are especially pertinent. They include a description of the personnel and curriculum of the black studies program. The pictorial likenesses of the black professors are a composite of the spiritual likeness of the man after whom the memorial chair was named. The mass of materials accumulating in the portfolios of the professors may well become the parchments of a developing black testament depicting the encounter between Martin Luther King, Jr., and his world.

The certain result of it all is the establishment of the effectiveness of the right to demand. Previously, when white chauvinism was confronted by nasty abrasion and caustic rejoinders, something close to bloodletting was apt to ensue. Today, where blacks find the nerve to submit to a correction of their image, they have the precedent of Martin Luther King, Jr., to hold up as an eternal catalyst. While obstacles still stand, they are not as obdurate as they once were. Walls can crumble without a resultant Samsonian chaos.

This is a new concept in the realm of racial strategy. The recalcitrance and vacillation of the power structures are now punctured by the prick of conscience sensitized by the thrust of the needle of compassion placed into black hands by the fundamental groundwork laid by the compassionate, Christlike, beleaguered martyr. The dimension of demand now rings with no accent of command, but rather with loving reprimand. King's redemptive death made palatable, if not completely acceptable, such substitute tactics in place of predatory demand. This is now a way of life for black people who see democracy as being invented for such a time and purpose as this.

The campaign of the black students to institute the program

of black studies at Rochester required the same pressure moves as those employed by the black caucus at the American Baptist Convention in Boston to present the name of the first black person to serve as president of the Convention. The contagion and stamina which gripped those involved in such campaigns came from the great dreamer. Willing catalysts all, they would not shirk the responsibilities which already had been borne by the prophet who, like his beloved Lord, was crucified upon the gibbet of racial discrimination and hatred. The Martin Luther King, Jr., Memorial Chair for Black Studies, and the whole department, point the way. May the pioneers of the program be thrice blessed as they witness the increase in their numbers!

Jesse
Jai
McNeil

HOW DARE HE!

Throughout black history and tradition in America, it has been usual for a black leader to be a preacher and pastor. But here was a man who stepped out beyond the usual incarceration to take a place in the world of Christian education. It was not because of any failure in the realm of preaching, for he had not failed. Sometimes it is said that a pharmacist is a frustrated medical school dropout or that an Episcopalian rector failed to become a Catholic priest because he failed his Latin. But Jesse Jai McNeil was neither frustrated nor a failure.

McNeil early saw that if the whole man in the church were to be served, he himself must be a whole man. If there was a paucity of black churchmen in the promising and burgeoning field of religious education, he was motivated to do his best to prepare black men to do that work. He must dip in his oar immediately, not waiting for the time when black churches would assert their readiness for such leadership. The fact that a few black constituencies being served by Caucasian directors of Christian education and musical directors are actually using

McNeil's methods and techniques lends solidity to the philosophy of this man.

Jesse Jai McNeil was born on February 24, 1913, in North Little Rock, Arkansas. He was one of a constellation of ten children. He was baptized when he was nine years old, and became a "boy preacher" at the age of thirteen.

There is a strange fascination at the thought of his middle name, Jai. It makes some "ouch" all over, and sets the speculative mind whirling. Is there no cue to its acquisition? His first name, Jesse, is no problem, for it is a good Bible name. But Jai! Why Jai? Is the name Irish or Scotch or, after the spirit of Gilbert and Sullivan in *H.M.S. Pinafore,* does it denote that Jesse was an Englishman? Or, to be phlegmatic, was his middle name a mere "J," a one-letter name which he later decided to spell out? Why this middle name was not in the typical black tradition of such as Johnson, Jackson, Brown, Green, or Smith does not matter; but the laconic staccato of "Jai" seems eminently right for one of his rare attainments because it is precisely as rare as its owner.

In appearance, he looked like somebody special. On a not-too-prominent nose were horn-rimmed glasses. A saucy moustache, just a tuft, sprouted over full lips that seemed to be straining to have a smile appear. A full covering of black, African hair exhibited no trace of gray. This was trained by comb, brush, hand, and skull cap, betraying the pomade era that cultivated the pompadour. A sturdy character was proclaimed by his round, symmetrical face. Nonetheless, out of it there shone the pride of achievement in himself and his offspring.

His death, on July 9, 1965, was called the "tragedy of the unfulfilled." Regardless of how well one qualifies for any task, it is inevitable that one day he must lay it down. His untimely death came just as he was approaching the peak of his professional development. Yet, he had destroyed the myth of black ineptitude in the spreading of the Word intelligently. Perhaps there had been more persuasive preachers and more imaginative pastors, but he knew no peer in the hitherto untried business of effective church leadership among blacks.

An evidence of God's further extravagance was Jesse's finding one who became his beloved wife, Pearl Lee Walker McNeil. It seemed to be a near perfect marriage. An undoubted help and inspiration to him before his death, she afterward directed student personnel at Bishop College. A rare spirit, she was elected as vice-president-at-large of the National Council of the Churches of Christ, was the author of the 1965 program for the World Day of Prayer, belongs to Zeta Phi Beta sorority, and appears in *Who's Who Among American Women*.

Four children are dazzling with promise. A report by Mrs. Elizabeth Haselden in the Kalamazoo *Baptist News,* vol. 14, no. 1, runs:

> Genna Rae McNeil of Dallas, Texas, was elected Homecoming Queen for 1968 by the student body and reigned over the festivities earlier this fall. Genna, an honor student and an outstanding member of the Senior Class, is the daughter of Mrs. Pearl Lee McNeil, Dean of Students at American Baptist Bishop College in Dallas. Her father, the late Jesse Jai McNeil, served for many years as Director of Publications for the National Baptist Convention and later was Professor of Christian Education at California Baptist Theological Seminary in Covina, California.

In addition, there is Jesse Jai McNeil, Jr., who became a music major and honor student at the University of Redlands; Kenneth Ross McNeil, who entered the United States Army; and Brenna Jean McNeil, who became a student at Bishop Dunn High School. In 1965, the two sons attended the Annual Congress of the National Baptist Convention, U.S.A., Incorporated, and, while there, made commitments to serve as foreign missionaries. All of his children rise up and call him blessed.

As a "boy wonder," Jesse could have gloried in the laurels heaped upon his head and relaxed in that kind of sunshine. But, wisely, he determined that he would go to college. He enrolled at Shurtleff College during the great depression. While in college, he served as pastor of a small congregation in East Alton, Illinois, the Tabernacle Baptist Church. From there, he went to the Graduate School of Religion of Virginia Union University and received the Bachelor of Divinity degree. Going on to Columbia University, he obtained the degrees of Bachelor of Science, Master of Arts, and Doctor of Education. He provided a topping with which to crown this educational cake by earning Certificates of Ecumenical Studies from Switzerland's Bossey and Celigny Institutes. If ever a soul brother was immersed in the brine of educational readiness, that person was Jesse Jai McNeil.

His education had prepared him to teach a "white man's" subject. Had he been white, his appointment as professor of Christian education at California Baptist Theological Seminary (now the American Baptist Seminary of the West, Covina Campus) would have been almost unnoticed. But a black man? A black man might have become a professor of preaching, but for him to be a professor of education caused pause! Where had he served an apprenticeship that prepared him to teach a white man's subject? In this chair, methods and principles, not charisma, would be his most important ingredient. Tools in the Christian education workshop are as indispensable as cadavers in the anatomy class. What could impel a big, grown man to fiddle with the likes of flannelgrams, visual aids, and role playing? It once was sarcastically said that all a Sunday school teacher needed was to learn how to operate a film projector. Cybernetics, computers, controlled data, punch cards, and programming, though fascinating, were considered as being for ladies, not for black preachers. Closed television and canned instruction may have been in the works for the morrow, but these should be left to women and frustrated male whites, who do not know how to preach, anyway.

ACHIEVEMENTS

McNeil's pastorates extended from strand to strand. New York's Salem Community Church and Pasadena's Metropolitan Baptist Church were at the coastal extremities; and between them were Nashville's Spruce Street Baptist Church and Detroit's prestigious Baptist Tabernacle, a truly noble charge. Weaving in unbroken pattern the threaded scarlet line of the pastoral fabric, he continued to engage in ministerial depth study to the end of his earthly ministry. Indeed, it was his quality of mind that prompted church committees to seek him out for their demanding pulpits.

The Sunday school has been called a necessary evil, an appendage, a superfluous adjunct to the main business of church. But men like McNeil have exploded any such theory by producing studies and books of high-quality research and biblical soundness. Reflected in his work as editor of Sunday school publications is an unmistakable commitment to Jesus Christ as Savior and Lord. His writings combine the stolid severity of oughtness with the filigree lacework of joyful reward so that they afforded the reader double value.

Perhaps McNeil's most impressive achievement was his appointment to the position of professor of Christian education at California Baptist Theological Seminary, at Covina, California. He had the distinction of being among the first of the black men to hold a significant position in a so-called white institution. Here he remained until his death.

Jesse was in demand for other positions of a volunteer nature. He was a leading spirit in the Annual Congress of the National Baptist Convention, U.S.A., Incorporated, which rivals its parent body in attendance, thousands of young people attending its sessions to learn and equip themselves for the work of Christian education in their local churches. He dreamed of the church that is to be and taught as if directors of Christian education were the vogue in all of the churches. A catalyst of God in an alien and untried wilderness, his too-early demise leaves men bewildered, but heartened that he left something significant for which to reach.

In 1963 he was on the platform of the American Baptist Convention as a panelist. This was the meeting in Detroit at which another prominent black leader, Ralph Bunche, was a featured speaker. McNeil's unusual competence when he brought cautious white Christians and eager black churchmen to a conference table in racially-troubled Detroit won him his spurs as a conciliator. Religious journals carried his lucid, challenging offerings which crossed denominational and racial lines. His trips overseas were frequent and, at a time when steamships carried most of the passengers, he was known as an international figure. As ubiquitous as a Baptist convention president, he covered his assignments with the dispatch of a diplomat, and wherever he went he left behind him goodwill in abundance. Both races deferred to him for his integrity and charisma. His brilliant leadership was left within and without the church.

McNeil believed in developing the art of writing, maintaining that it was as important as the art of speaking. Whether he was writing books or producing materials for use in the church school, he regarded himself as reaching his readers by a meaningful mode of expression of the ministry. In 1960, the William B. Eerdmans Publishing Company brought out his book *As Thy Days, So Thy Strength*. He was then one of a few black preachers to have his work published by a large commercial publisher. A glance at the title suggests that the book is a series of inspirational tidbits fashioned to tide the reader over his day-by-day pitfalls. But the book is much more than this. Heavily documented with Scripture, as well as other reference material, McNeil sets forth his ponderous Christian educational theories, setting them in the christological framework of a critical theologian. Neither spicy nor "cute," the content is quite removed from the shallow cheer which the title might at first suggest.

In 1961, under the auspices of the same publisher, *The Minister's Service Book for Pulpit and Parish* appeared. Like the *Minister's Service Book* by James Dalton Morrison, it was a considerable improvement over the old, outdated Hiscox *Star Book*. Its timeliness and excellence assured it a place on the library shelves of many black and white pastors.

Also in 1961, his book entitled *The Preacher-Prophet in Mass Society* appeared. Like the foregoing, it was published by the William B. Eerdmans Publishing Company, of Grand Rapids.

Moments in His Presence then appeared, again published by Eerdmans in 1962. He prepared this volume especially to fill a need resulting from the starchiness and unrelatedness of other extant day-by-day devotional books. Preachers in unsophisticated black churches, who, nevertheless, regarded their books with pride and had but limited fondness for breakfast interruptions, found that this book greatly satisfied their needs.

Published in 1965, his next book, *Mission in Metropolis*, reflected the clamor, confusion, din, turmoil, and squalor of the muck that is characteristic of the large city in modern America. This book was contemporaneous with *The Secular City* by Harvey Cox. It is a thrilling and clear call for workers to do their Christian gleaning in the forbidding fields of the "asphalt jungles of America."

One more book deserves listing here. It was entitled *Men in the Local Church*, published by the Sunday School Board of the National Baptist Convention, U.S.A., Incorporated, in Nashville.

To grasp McNeil's material, the reader had to think, a process that was consistent with his philosophy of work. If his content proved to be obscure on occasion, it was only because the Scriptures themselves contained passages that were obdurate and strange. One so benighted as to believe that ignorance and Negritude were synonymous would have been delivered from such colossal bondage if he had first known Jesse Jai McNeil.

PHILOSOPHY

When Jesse Jai McNeil went home to his Maker, he had packed into his fifty-two years a life-style befitting the finest any man could vouchsafe to posterity. From whatever perspective one evaluates this life, he will find that the whole sweep of the teaching-learning spectrum is contained. The piercing light that fractured the prism of his thought-crowned mind spells Christianity. Herein lies his greatness.

McNeil's writings were published during the first five years of the 1960s, assuring that his contributions are still fresh and relevant. It was not for the black church, but for the Protestant church that he wrote; but his emphasis upon Christian education bore heavily upon an area of critical need in the churches of the black community. Black Baptist churches are pulpit centered; McNeil was desirous that they become classroom-oriented, study-conscious. Black churches soberly call their pastors, but they merely look around for some willing man, regardless of his training, to man the Christian education leadership barracks. McNeil would make the Christian educator a part of a team, associated with the pastor. He further considered the posts of counselor and minister of music as major ministries. In the black church, such functionaries are either optional or nonexistent. Whereas black churches tend to construct their educational plants first, then fashion their programs, McNeil would first determine the program, then build an edifice to accommodate it.

McNeil's emphasis upon religious education, which he preferred to call Christian education, was a part of his innovative approach of giving catholicity to the ministry. He saw the ministry as proceeding along many avenues, of which pulpit oratory was only one. With such depth of perspective, its attractiveness was enhanced in the eyes of eager, but pulpit-shy, youth as they realized that there were kinds of service to the church which might well bring out the best that was in them.

McNeil pleaded for the comprehensive application of the gospel in all human situations. However, the black churches seemed to miss the point of this principle. Their educational plants permitted little or none of the usual forms of recreation; there were only the Baptist Training Union or the Baptist Youth Fellowship — and perhaps an occasional league basketball game.

EVALUATION

Jesse Jai McNeil was called by many names. He was said to be an intellectual giant, a clean writer, a social engineer, and a successful parent. At the obsequies, Dr. D. C. Washington described him as a "man of vision." Dr. Horace N. Mays, the brilliant Christian educator in his own right, extolled his virtues, naming him *"The* Christian Educator." The words from the numerous and august body of speakers at the funeral service were inadequate to set forth the true glory and majestic dignity of the man, whose very name — Jesse Jai McNeil — seemed to be surcharged with added significance by that one and only middle name.

McNeil's central concern in his writing, his preaching, his deliberations on boards, and his teaching was his intense dedication to the cause of Jesus Christ. He saw his task as that of an interpreter, that is, to set forth with crystal clarity what Christian education was all about. Through this discipline he would be instrumental in changing the lives of all with whom he came in contact.

McNeil's appointment to a professorship at California raises a vexing question. There were other such appointments. Drew Theological Seminary long since held George D. Kelsey as one of its cherished faculty members. The Methodists had procured the services of Howard Thurman and John Satterwhite for

Boston University and Wesley Theological Seminary, respectively. Theodore Jones was called to Crozer Theological Seminary, and Henry Mitchell has been serving at Colgate Rochester Divinity School. What are black seminaries going to do in the light of the depressing phenomenon which is currently called "the brain drain"? Are they to become ecclesiastical stepchildren in the competition between institutions? Within the context of religion, this state of affairs is an anomaly, for traditionally the black Baptists have immersed themselves in religion, embracing and grasping it as if it were the "balm in Gilead."

There are corollaries to this question. One lies in the question as to whether, at last, it seems to be the right and proper thing to hire only black professors for black institutions, and only white professors for white institutions. Under such black separatism, when a black man steps out of a situation, he is replaced by a white man; and vice versa. This is another form of the brain drain.

Perhaps as men eulogize the Jesse Jai McNeils and watch the more affluent institutions skim off from the top the best brains of either race, we are also watching as the black institutions become the havens of the mediocre.

The black man's greatest gift is the power to become. But the black man often eschews the gift, saying, with the cynic, "The leopard cannot change his spots." Long ago a wise writer said, "Beloved, we are God's children now; it does not yet appear what we shall be, but we know that when he appears we shall be like him, for we shall see him as he is" (1 John 3:2, RSV). Like *him*, not like leopards. Some, like Ananias and Sapphira, want prestige without paying the price. But, thank God, under the determination to cope and to persevere, many a black ministerial student has qualified for vocational acceptance and excellence, despite the paucity of supportive financial props to sustain him academically.

Jesse Jai McNeil lived and spoke for the highest ideals in Christian living and thinking. Who shall replace a person like this? The demand for dignity and worth is in the land. Who will prepare the ground, that the seedlings of potential greatness may germinate? McNeil's article, "The Next Years for the Director of Christian Education," appearing posthumously in

101

The Baptist Teacher magazine (Fall, 1965), reveals the director in reasonably human terms. The author's rebukes were gentle and his scholarship was high. McNeil himself was his own greatest achievement. From him emanated the rapier-like thrusts of a philosophic mind and the generosity of a great soul whose bloodline went back to the American system of chattel slavery.

May the time be close at hand when the spontaneity and discipline represented in the works and life of Jesse Jai McNeil combine to produce men and women of God, approved ones who have no need to be ashamed, rightly handling the word of truth (see 2 Timothy 2:15).

James Everett Rose

A cub of a man, short and stocky, who waddled like some Friar Tuck, stood in the great pulpit of the silk-stockinged Mount Olivet Baptist Church in Rochester, New York. His mien gave evidence of his inflation almost to the point of pomposity, whatever discernible sprig of humility being confined to the proportions of a tender bud. Yet as he lashed out against inhumanity and unfairness, his appearance was wondrously forgotten, for here was a man of education, erudition, and eloquence. One of God's "Bad Boys," James Everett Rose ascended from his origin as the grandson of a slave to make his mark in the world.

MEETING THE WORLD

James Everett Rose was born on January 3, 1883, in Centralia, Virginia. Poverty was no stranger to most black families, and it was a perennial adversary in the rural environs where the Rose family lived. The anguish and struggle of his boyhood were remembered throughout his life; agonized tales of woe from his early years appeared in his pulpit discourses.

He was determined to be somebody. If this were to happen, he instinctively knew that he must both go to college and consummate a strategic and successful marriage. He achieved his first goal by attending Howard University; then he went on to Rochester Theological Seminary. There he met and became a close friend of Mordecai Wyatt Johnson, another student at the seminary and pastor of the Second Baptist Church in nearby Mumford, New York. Johnson later became president of Howard University.

THE LOVED ONES

While at Howard University, James Rose had met Mamie Reddy, of Beton, South Carolina, born on March 9, 1888. They were married in 1915, and together they attacked the work at Leroy, New York, then considered as a mission work, not far from Rochester. Here a lively literary club preempted the place usually occupied by a weekly prayer meeting. Before long, the mission became the Second Baptist Church of Leroy. Grievously, the marriage was a short one, for the rigors of the grim winters that are characteristic of that part of the country caught up with Mamie, and she expired in December, 1919, only a little over four years after her marriage.

On March 18, 1892, four hundred years after Columbus discovered America, Carrie Louise Dukes was born. She was destined to become Rose's second wife. After graduating from Spelman College in the class of 1915, she became a pioneer among people of her race in the professional practice of social work. This marriage was indeed a fortunate one for James Rose, for Carrie virtually carried him, not back to "Ol' Virginny," but on to renown and glory as one of the race's ablest intellectual preachers.

Eventually James and Carrie were blessed by the birth of two sons; the home was "girlless." James Everett Rose III was born on August 26, 1922, and is a dentist. Cornelius Harreld Rose arrived about two years later, on April 26, 1924. He is following in the footsteps of his mother in the field of professional social work.

To complete the family picture, one more person came into the home during the Rochester years. Hovering about the Rose family with a devotion befitting one who literally worshiped the head of the household was the lady named Miss Emma Marrow.

106

Her ties with the family have never clearly been explained, but her spiritual right to a place in the family could hardly be gainsaid. This gentle, capable soul walked in strong quietness, in the dignified assurance of her self-won esteem as a member of the Rose family tradition.

Without any apparent indication of formal schooling, Emma Marrow was one of education's strongest supporters. In order to attain competence and ability to perform successfully as a church worker, she attended classes, meetings, and all such groups as might help her to improve. Consequently, she was a first-class Sunday school teacher, an effective leader in the Baptist Training Union, and the quintessence of excellence in missionary leadership and all-around public relations. Her place in the Rose home was no mere appendage, but was like one ventricle of a great heart beating in concert to make a contribution of healing and helping. She was indeed an important part of the total heart thrust whose pulsations could be heard and felt throughout the Mount Olivet community.

When he died, she died. One of the poignant remembrances of events at the funeral service was the completely resigned look upon the countenance of Emma Marrow, from which, along with Sister Carrie's, all the sparkle had been drained. A short time later she expired.

THE PASTOR

Of the Mount Olivet Baptist Church, Rochester, the executive secretary of the Baptist Union of Rochester and Monroe County said, "It is the most impressive Negro church on the New York Central Railroad between New York and Chicago." Few who are acquainted with the circumstances would be inclined to disagree.

Many of the buildings used by urban blacks are discards that have been abandoned by whites in the wake of their speedy exit to suburbia. American culture runs that way. But, contrary to the pattern, James Rose led his congregation in the erection of a magnificent, functional Gothic building. It was new, from the ground up. The cruciform-shaped plan served as a worship center and provided for an educational plant to be added later. Herein developed the fulfillment of his fondest dream — to build

the kind of church structure whose rest rooms were located somewhere other "than under the front steps leading down to the
basement." The inclusion of a three-manual pipe organ gives
a better clue to the affluent equipment that was characteristic
of the plant. One is led to wonder what were the magic words
used to persuade the members to plunge into such a venture of
faith, rather than to obey the visionless dictation of the habitual
and mundane "in" thing.

To some, the church appeared to be out of character, with a
black snob, an "uppity Negro," for a preacher. Even when its
record proved otherwise, the church never lived down its repu-
tation as a place that harbored snooty colored folks who liked
to associate with white folks. After all, was not its first organist
white? And did it not have a white person on the board of
deaconesses? And what about that white preacher from the
German seminary who was ordained there? And so it went.

Supposedly, there was a price to be paid for the warm welcome extended to Henry Burke Robins, the philosopher, who
was a frequent visitor, and for the regular attendance of Hallie
Poteat, the seminary president's daughter, not to mention the
frequent attendance of the president himself, the renowned
Edwin McNeill Poteat.

In addition to carrying on a carefully contrived program,
attested to by a file of printed bulletins, there were trained
musicians, and the choir and congregation engaged in the singing
of choral responses and antiphonal exercises. This great church
served also as a field-work center for black students at the
seminary. It was then the only one that did so. The names of
those who received such unusual schooling comprise a veritable
who's who in black church leadership in America. Short-lived, but
memorable, were most of the ties that bound James Rose to a
long troop of student assistants, from Howard Thurman to
Charles Boddie. The list includes the names of Joseph Harrison
Jackson, Wade Hampton McKinney, Lloyd Hickman, James
Timothy Boddie, and Charles Saulter. How fortunate it was for
this writer that the fellowship that was forged among us held
long after the glue had hardened!

Famous musicians were associated with the activities. Some
of the luminaries from the star-studded Eastman School of Music

were Kenneth Spencer, Robert Warfield, Mark Fax, and Joan Salmon — to name just a few. The highly esteemed assets of this rare cultural stronghold were solidly appropriated by this imaginative upstate New York congregation.

The achievements of James Rose as pastor of the Mount Olivet Baptist Church became his hallmark of greatness. A staunch believer in education, he married two college-educated wives. At a time when it was a rarity to find many black youths who could boast even a high school diploma, this pastor claimed several college-bred young people in his congregation. He abhorred ignorance and whatever bedeviling influence there was that led unenlightened minds to glorify it. The grandson of a slave, he would not be suspected of setting out to repair the lugubrious image of the ungrammatical, unlearned preacher man, the crude babbler who was at one with John Jasper propounding that "the sun do move." That he did so was no mystery when it is discovered that he held academic degrees from Howard University and Virginia Union University and was one of very few who received an earned graduate degree from the Colgate Rochester Divinity School.

The Mount Olivet Baptist Church had been founded by Charles D. Hubert, of Morehouse College fame. When the great Dr. Hubert decided to return to Georgia and his first love — teaching — James Rose was called to the pastorate. The church was made to order for him. Here was a climate in which Rose's penchant for education and erudition could thrive. He was surrounded by college-trained spouses and the silk-stockinged (black American bourgeois) constituency. The fact that Rochester was in those days an artisan's, rather than a proletarian's, bailiwick aided and abetted the cause and case for intellectual pursuit. Another might have found the heritage of the depression years unbearable. Yet, on a salary of $1800 a year, he matched the onslaught of despair with an optimism and faith not known before in Israel.

At first glance, one could hardly believe that Rose possessed a flair for the aesthetic, especially in the forms of dramatics and literature, in which he frequently indulged with an uncommon degree of expertise and repartee. In the pulpit, Paul Laurence Dunbar sprang to life, and the likes of G. A. Studdert-Kennedy and John Oxenham were conjured up to soothe the more sophisticated brow. Also, he wrote good poetry and dabbled in the realm of producing biblical scenes for dramatic and musical productions in which his thespians and singers in the church membership might be encouraged — or impelled — to turn a dollar or two into the till. Every penny was baptized during the bleak depression days.

He was under the illusion that he possessed a fine singing voice. The writer, just starting his own ministry under him, was in no position to refuse when he offered his bass contribution to the choir. But Rose did much better when he was duetting with his wife, Carrie, especially when the levity of "Rachel, Rachel, I've Been Thinking" was spicing a church social function!

THE STENTORIAN ROAR

In the pulpit and out of it, the consuming urge of James Rose was to exalt the black man. This he did defiantly in the face of the racism of the well-meaning but naïve municipality. Above all, he did not deserve the accusation made by another prominent black man that he was "whitey's placater." But epithets flung at him and at his own ethnic kin were foreign to his way and spirit. He was a gentleman, and as such he maintained a dignity and refinement that would not permit him to stoop to the use of onerous references to "whitey" and "honkey."

James Rose was foremost in the rights struggle of his day in Rochester. The year 1954 marked the turning point in the black man's quest for self-realization. The ruling by the United States Supreme Court outlawing school segregation divided the black man's time as, long before, time had been divided into B.C. and A.D. Thirty years before this momentous event, the consuming passion of black leaders had been to bring about the passage of the Dyer Bill. This bill called for the abolishment of the hideous practice of lynching blacks in the southern part of the land. It has become all but lost for years in the legislative history of the struggle of the black man for his total emancipation.

The power and influence of James Rose in Rochester during the early days of the thirties was staggering. The stentorian roar

110

from his raucous, gravelly throat is still unforgettable. There are those who can still feel the pulpit shake under his tremulous outpourings. They still see the thick, rotund neck supporting a roundish, bowling-ball head, with hair parted carefully on the side, and with a proud, forward face jutting out in front, bearing trembling lips which snarled out toilsome barbs against those who persecuted his people, who disinherited them, and who rendered them exploitable by the blandishments of irrepressible and short-sighted prejudice fostered by bigoted, money-mad economic pundits whose word on policy and political matters in the blackless, back smoke-filled rooms was the law. Unlike his friend Mordecai Johnson, who strode from one end of the platform to the other, James Rose stood stark, flatfootedly still; but with his eyes rolling in a frenzy, his nostrils dilating, and perspiration oozing from every pore in his quivering body, he rang the verbal changes upon all who would deprive his people of the right to have, to belong, and to be. The wise race baiter did well to flee before his acrid, unrelenting invective. And when was he not on such a prowl?

Perhaps no man ever lashed out against the evil of lynching as he did. The unusual event of a white man being lynched provoked him to preach a sermon entitled "It Is Wrong to Lynch — *Some* People." In a devastating tirade, he exploded in a pulpit vendetta on the evil of lynching that reverberated on into the present and future! In contrast to the acquittal which usually followed that foul method of murdering black men, the leader of the mob was condemned to death. That sermon still rings in the ears of this writer!

Were he to return and witness the holocaust of confusion on today's college campuses he would be horrified, for the height of his youthful ambition was to attain his hard-earned and pridefully regarded college education. He would not be able to understand those (especially black young people) who scorn the chance to learn, to earn, and to own by paying through their noses, if need be, for the right to come by the great blessings of education by the dint and discipline of hard work and study.

Not every moment of his life was free from the carrying of a heavy burden. A sorry episode is an example. It took place while James Rose was the honored moderator of the Baptist Union of

Monroe County. As such, he was invited to attend a significant dinner. A high-ranking church official from the South was invited to the same dinner. Shame and remorse gripped the entire dining room of the Hotel Seneca when the visiting cleric refused to enter, for fear that he might have to sit at the table with the other special guest, Dr. James E. Rose. On that tragic evening both men went hungry; one for want of knowledge of the ways of stodgy reactionary habit, and the other for want of the milk of common, decent, human kindness. James Rose, naïve in his innocence, and the other, stiff-necked in his prejudice, caused ghosts to come alive. All were sick.

The drama of that night would have stirred another great man into action. Frederick Douglass had resided in Rochester and had been editor of *The North Star,* which was published from the basement of a nearby Methodist church. Surely, the statue that was there erected to his memory stirred a bit, as it was silhouetted against the skyline; and his body in an adjacent grave must have tilted slightly, along with those of the blessed band whose bones in all likelihood rattled ever so lightly in that section reserved in the Mount Hope Cemetery for the heroes of the Underground Railroad. The great orator and friend of Abraham Lincoln would certainly have had something juicy to write about had he been privy to that heartbreaking event on that melancholy evening.

Rose's interfaith ties were as strong as his interracial ones. Rabbi Philip Bernstein, Archbishop James Kearney, and Hugh Chamberlain Burr of the Protestant Federation of Churches all felt a brotherly kinship with James Rose. His ability to parlay the eclectic mishmash from the potpourri of heterogeneous ecumenicity and focus it into a concentrate for brotherly understanding in the common foray against prejudice and racism marks him as a man of distinction. In a city renowned for its grass-roots solidarity and close-knit ethnic association, he proved to be the man for all seasons.

If the nation is any better in matters of race, no Rochesterean of that day or any day is more responsible for it than James Rose. In the events of his life one finds the genesis of the concerted fight for justice for Rochester's black citizens which finds its present counterpart in the movement named FIGHT under the leadership of Franklin Florence and organized with the help of the late Saul Alinsky.

Rose was a black John Brown, God's angry man who put his wrath to redemptive work, dynamiting the darkness, disdaining the predatory utterance, and, instead, performing the pragmatic deed.

To say that all these advancements in Rochester could have occurred without the impact of James Rose would be like saying that the Negro slave could have been physically emancipated without the person of Abraham Lincoln. The aura of events and opportunities that characterize the life-style and ambitions of James Rose bear that consistently high degree of excellence that is ever at war to the death against the mediocre, the trivial, and the decadent.

For twenty-one years, James Rose labored from the vantage point of pastor, preacher, civil servant, and counselor. All of these were forged into a ministry of reconciliation which transformed the life of the black people in the sophisticated city of Rochester.

PLAUDITS

To this man came the simultaneous honors of being elected to the board of trustees of Howard University and having bestowed upon him the honorary degree of Doctor of Divinity. These honors, coming in 1940, comprised the capstone of his unusual career, for he had but two more years to live. The merited honor took into account the meticulous care and faithful persistence in building a quality church and high-grade program from a meager and unpromising beginning. It attested to his presence in a proud American city as no mere fleshy reference point to salve the consciences of the members of the establishment to which he belonged, but whose very conscience he himself had become. Howard University was taking full cognizance of his place in the affairs of Rochester as one of the city fathers who was sensitive to the needs of his lesser black brothers. The act of honoring him in this way was his alma mater's wager that what had been accomplished through his efforts was a harbinger of greater things to come.

Albert W. Beaven, for many years pastor of the Lake Avenue

113

Baptist Church and the first president of Colgate Rochester Divinity School after its merger, was one of James Rose's staunchest admirers. So was Clarence Barbour, one-time president of Brown University. When they called him "Jim," it had a regal sound. There was no hint of "boy" in it.

Nor did the plaudits come only from clergymen. In the admiring crowd around him were Alfred Hart, a well-known grocer; Mrs. Harper Sibley, a churchwoman known around the world; John Remington, a noted jurist and venerable and Baptist to the core; and Frank Gannett, the wry, gnarled Unitarian who owned both of Rochester's newspapers. These all shared Jim's passion for a peaceable kingdom.

The writer's first contact with the Rose family was a meeting with the Roses' five-year-old son, Cornelius Harreld. Sitting on the porch steps of the Edinburgh Street frame house, he answered my query about the whereabouts of his father by proudly pointing his finger upstairs. Our small talk bound us in thrall when we discovered that we were both products of parsonages, and our dads were something special. Scaling the steps two at a time, I entered half nervously and half boldly into the presence of the courteous, yet severe and foreboding, man, whose ice melted the very second I introduced myself. He knew and respected my father; and he had just shed himself of my big brother, Tim, who had graduated from Colgate Rochester Divinity School and was a pastor in Lackawanna, New York. I explained that I was a basketball player, in town to do battle with the all-black West Side Y team. Before I left, he made the implausible prediction that I would be back on a more important mission than that of representing the Syracuse Dunbars' basketball team.

And how right he was! Let the record show that in September, 1933, I registered as a young theologue at the Colgate Rochester Divinity School and carried out my field apprenticeship under him at his church. Further, in July, 1942, I was called to be the pastor of the Mount Olivet Baptist Church of Rochester — to catch the mantle of the patron saint of black Rochester.

The privilege of organizing the ROSE MEMORIAL FELLOWSHIP was undertaken as a labor of love. Its mission might well be to try to temper the rising tides of racial misunderstanding by reminding the denizens of Kodaktown of the contributions of James Rose to the peace and stability of the city of Rochester. One does not use the word "tranquillity" in connection with him, for he was a stormy petrel. May the ROSE MEMORIAL FELLOWSHIP call to the attention of the black students and professors now at the Divinity School the remembrance of that "bad boy" who walked in this town and land, putting sinew into the civil rights movement long before it came to be known by that name, who was no Uncle Tom, but whose critical loyalty helped to keep a whole community from going racially "haywire," holding up the ridgepole of hope along the banks of the Genesee.

His likeness is preserved in an appropriate portrait which hangs in the vestibule of his beloved church, where men of all races, faiths, and climes worship God together.

Marshall L.
Shepard, Sr.

Man of monstrous mirth, he was the shepherd who captured both hearts and votes. Plump, brown, and laughingly round, this man of charm, buoyancy, and radiance not only made those around him feel good, but they were good to him. Because, in their eyes, he was truly great, they saved him from condemnation to the mediocrity of being called just a "nice guy." They called him "Shep." As only about one-sixth of an iceberg is visible above the surface of the water, this account can reveal only about one-sixth of what might be said about Marshall L. Shepard, Sr.

RARE HUMAN

Marshall L. Shepard, Sr., was born in Oxford, North Carolina, to the late Robert and Pattie Gilliam Shepard, on July 10, 1899. In his native town, he discovered Miss Lucille Owens, and the couple were united in marriage in 1923. In due time, two sons were born. Notwithstanding the strenuous career that Marshall maintained, he was a good husband and father in the home. This father deserves resounding hallelujahs for so bringing up these boys that, when the proper time arrived, they responded to the call to enter the pastoral ministry as a viable career. In a magnificent commitment to which few fathers are privileged to bear witness, these two sons honor their pastor-father's memory in offering themselves as living monuments to the validity and authenticity of their earthly father's example. Imagine the force of the celestial clout when two lives of one's own flesh and blood are thus dedicated!

Shepard was one of a family that was rich in educators, teachers, and preachers. An uncle, James Shepard, founder and president of what is now North Carolina Central University, in Durham, was especially attached to his nephew. He lavished every possible advantage upon him, and much of Shep's success is traceable to this generous assistance. James Shepard's activity had run the gamut of many varieties of human service. The younger Shepard touched bases at a majority of the points where his Uncle Jim previously had held forth, gaining prominence in most and eminence in some. Bound to such an affluent and benevolent sponsor, the relationship was of such closeness as to make it seem more appropriate to say "Like father, like son," than "Like uncle, like nephew." With his Uncle Jim's person, purse, and prayers ever by his side, how could Shep keep from aspiring in all ways to be like him?

Marshall's religious experience began in his early life in Oxford, where he accepted Christ as his Savior and was baptized in the First Baptist Church. Later, in the same church, he was licensed to preach. Also, in the same church he was ordained to the ministry.

His early education took place at the Slater Normal and Industrial School, from which he graduated. From thence, he went to Virginia Union University, Richmond, Virginia, receiving the Bachelor of Arts degree. For discipline in theology, he attended Union Theological Seminary, New York. Still further studies were pursued at Pendle Hill, Wallingford, Pennsylvania, and at Temple University, Philadelphia, Pennsylvania. Beyond this impressive formal education, he received numerous honorary degrees.

His official ministry began with a three-year tenure as assistant pastor of the Abyssinia Baptist Church in New York City. In 1926 he accepted the call to the pulpit of the Mount Olivet Tabernacle Baptist Church, in Philadelphia, where he remained for more than forty years, ending only with his passing from this life on February 21, 1967.

Shepard's vast reservoir of power was to pour forth through several channels, his humane services covering a variety of occupations, including social work, politics, denominational leadership, and statesmanship. He held many offices of trust and honor, among which were Religious Work Secretary at the Harlem YMCA, chairman of the Foreign Mission Board of the National Baptist Convention, U.S.A., Incorporated; delegate to and speaker at the Baptist World Alliance; member of the Board of Directors of the Christian Street YMCA, Philadelphia, Pennsylvania; committee member of the Division of Christian Life and Work of the National Council of the Churches of Christ in the United States of America; member of the Board of Directors of the Bureau for Child Care in Philadelphia; and member of the Board of Directors of the United Fund of Greater Philadelphia.

In rallying his attributes into full use for all people, this personable dynamo revealed the stern stuff of which some human beings are made. He was not given to a mere passing interest in social work, but he was the founder of service clubs and occupied important seats on the boards of social service organizations. He did not simply dabble a little in politics, but he won elections and received important federal, state, and municipal appointments. He was no ordinary delegate to the National Baptist Convention, U.S.A., Incorporated, but was a selected one to occupy the post of chairman of the Board of Foreign Missions. He was not just another young theologue in Union Theological Seminary, but, while there, he was an assistant pastor in the world's largest black church.

By his gift of versatility, he was valuable to his voting constituents and, at the same time, vulnerable to the complaints of his parishioners, for he served people who were at once a body of franchised ballot holders and a gathering of church members. In the midst of his profusion of activity, he seemed to maintain a relationship with a people who were gradually becoming aroused, be they his electors or his parishioners.

He was able to put all things together so well that President Franklin D. Roosevelt found him to be the one man he needed in a special situation. At the Democratic Convention, when it looked as though all unity was trickling away through the dike that was breached by racism, Roosevelt sought to shore up the waters by having Shep lead the convention in prayer. As he rose to pray, "Cotton Ed" Smith, of South Carolina, stalked from the hall. "What did you think?" queried an anxious delegate of Shep. He replied: "That just goes to show you how badly we all need prayer!" and, eyes twinkling, he bounded merrily on his way.

How well he quelled the fires of bigotry is impossible to say, but undoubtedly his swagger could "con" as well as charm. Even when a victim of his knew that he was being taken, the jovial stealth of the portly black Falstaff was not resented. Indeed, his wily machinations helped to increase the number of his admirers.

Shepard's view from the pastorate in Philadelphia gave him a sharp awareness of the crying needs of the black people in his community. His consequent decision to attempt to meet these needs by way of the political route was justified by repeated successful elections to public office. Finally, he was propelled into the legislature of the commonwealth of Pennsylvania where, for three terms, he made the arduous trips between his Philadelphia parsonage and the Harrisburg legislative halls.

After his years in the legislature, the president appointed him as the Recorder of Deeds for Washington, D.C. During that time, he and Mary McLeod Bethune were the only black servants of the government on assignment in Washington. He resigned from this position in 1951, in order to run for election as Recorder of Deeds for the city of Philadelphia. Needless to say, he won. When, in 1953, there was a reorganization in which two departments were merged, he was named Commissioner of Records.

Continuing in the Philadelphia scene, he became a nominee for councilman-at-large in 1955. He was elected to that office in the November election and served in it throughout the rest of his days.

Shepard's ability as a statesman stood him in good stead in his denominational work which, in turn, took him beyond the borders of his own nation. His position as chairman of the Board of Foreign Missions of the National Baptist Convention, U.S.A., Incorporated, increased his already rich largesse of world entrepreneurship. From this stance, he was able to interpret the meaning of the emergence of African political structures which were on their way to reaching full stature as objects of primary importance in the counsels of the United Nations. His acquaintance with important African leaders and his extensive overseas travel firmly established his prestige as an international personage. The relevant work of his board, whose main area of participation was Africa, helped to weld under his touch both missions and international affairs into an exciting church-state adventure. He was one of the most traveled, worldly wise individuals in America.

TRIBAL CHIEF

To the members of the Mount Olivet Tabernacle Baptist Church, the Reverend Marshall L. Shepard, Sr., was the esteemed shepherd of the flock into which they were gathered with a most tender benignancy. Understandably, his congregation did not pin the laconic label "Shep" upon him. Despite the variety of other preoccupations in which he was engaged, it seemed to many that he expended all his love and energy upon his congregation.

Aside from the versatility which the helpful influence of his uncle-benefactor inspired, the young pastor mastered the art of adaptability and learned how to profit from its execution. In his ghetto ministry, Shep soon found that any member who was plagued by a pressing need would invariably turn to the pastor for help. Customarily and inevitably, countless assignments of this nature have been imposed upon the prestige personality, the tribal chief, the black pastor, who, to this day, stands in the ghetto as liaison between his brothers in need and the establishment, supervising when opportunity indicates, improvising when necessity dictates. Thus, the black pastor is compelled to recognize his responsibility for dealing with the stringencies of black-ghetto living, with its attendant mind-shattering, heartbreaking frustrations. Should sensitivity be lacking here, he is a failure.

Almost instinctively, Shep developed the art of dispensing help. He knew the precious value of genuine friendship, and especially the privilege of being a friend to those who were most in need. Perhaps the qualities were aided by his happy experience with Uncle Jim, from whom he learned how graciously to accept aid.

Through more than forty years, Marshall's cardinal concern was his pastorate. His attention to his church was both diligent and sacrificial. One of the most effective reliefs from the pressures that bedevil the black pastor is the acquisition of a prestigious pastorate. Marshall found the one that captured his heart when he went to the Mount Olivet Tabernacle Baptist Church. Once settled down into this satisfying situation, he was well on his way.

Here, parenthetically, we might stop to play with words. If the expression "settled down" does not match with the expression "on his way," perhaps a more dramatic way of describing Shep is that he "took off!" In the settling down process, he attended to all the chores peculiar to a ghetto charge: pastoral calls, hospital visitation, the solemnization of marriages, and the burial of the dead. While he was doing these things, he was also "taking off" in the many avenues of ventures which already have been described.

Building upon his accomplishments in Harlem as a community worker and his pioneer pastoral ministry which partially manifested itself in the erection of an educational building for his Philadelphia parishioners, he became active in a myriad of ghetto-serving projects. A mosaic of deep need, even in that day, reflected the melancholy times. The drug habit was already casting its hideous blight upon the lives of black youth. Ministering to them in their heartrending predicament was a task not unknown to Shep. He had rightly come by his spurs in the field of social work.

As a youth, I had personal experience with this warmhearted human being. One Sunday, at Shep's invitation, three of us journeyed to Philadelphia to serve his congregation. Pop preached, Dick timorously sang, and the author accompanied his brother on the piano and fearfully coaxed the organ. Shep's kind of indulgence of the effort put out by the boys bespoke the patience and understanding of one who himself had negotiated similarly troubled waters, perhaps as director of the Junior Hi Y fledglings when, stretching their wings, the genius of his charges was revealing itself for the first time. No apologies for the visiting preacher were needed; but there is no doubt that Shep's concern for the beginners who stood only at the threshold of usefulness and self-discovery, giving out musically on that hot, humid August Sunday afternoon, had just as sympathetically extended itself to countless other fourteen-year-old boys. It was a Sunday to remember.

COMPELLING PREACHER

As is the case with the others of God's "bad boys" in this volume, the reason Marshall L. Shepard, Sr., is included in this constellation is that he was a preacher. Dr. George A. Buttrick has said that, on the average, the minimal time required for the constructing of a good sermon is fourteen hours. Assuming this to be a thoughtful estimate and remembering the numerous activities in which Shep was constantly engaged, one wonders when he found the time for preparation. Perhaps the answer comes easily when it becomes known that Dr. Gardner Taylor, one of Shep's closest friends, called Marshall Shepard "probably the best extemporaneous preacher that the black race has produced."

He made hundreds of visitations to the preaching stations of his peers and colleagues, joining their celebrations, observing their anniversaries, leading their revival services, and sharing their joys and sorrows. The very enormity of it all grimly overtaxed him. How he managed to cover it all remains a mystery.

REVIEW OF A COUNSELOR

Marshall Shepard retained complete and simultaneous possession of two long-term attachments: his church pastorate and his councilmanic seat. The congregation upheld his shepherding arms and the voters preserved his political eminence. What undergirded this close relationship between parson and person is not clear. It is apparent, however, that today something is happening to destroy this state of mutuality. Because the challenge to examine the reasons for such disintegration has become so insistent, it is the burden of this story to study Shepard's success more closely.

In the final tribute to Marshall L. Shepard, Sr., the usual phrases of adulation are written into his obituary. Under the circumstances, of course, the accolades are acceptable. However, the haunting question arises: How, in the hardheaded and exacting crucible of today's abrasive mind set, would such an obituary fare? Would the survivors hold as praiseworthy the suspicion that an adequate service to their kind of church had been hobbled by their pastor's preoccupation with outside commitments of a nonreligious nature? Given today's rigid demands of the pastorate, would the Mount Olivet Tabernacle Baptist Church so readily and supinely again assume the springboard stance? Would a winsome, magnetically attractive life-style of a popular pastor suffice to contain a rising tide of criticism against him for the diverting of his gifts to other than parish-oriented involvement? It is more likely that an updated profile on Shep would appear considerably dissimilar to the actual understanding which he then had with the pulpit committee. Should there be no change from Shep's style in the ministerial pattern of some contemporary pastor, might it not be expected that there would be bleats of consternation from the stalls of the sheep?

There are more questions to be considered. Are today's ministries within the domain of the black church so pressure-packed as to require the full-time attention of the pastor? Was it normative in Shepard's time for the black preacher to regard a "call" as related only to parish duties? Is there ever a time when the preacher's circumstances might justifiably have permitted a conjunction of his job as pastor with other jobs connected to mundane affairs? Should the so-called secular pursuits ever be placed under the rubrics of pastoral responsibility? Can one fairly invoke a plea for moderation of occupational expansion on the sheer grounds of regard for one's health? In the preacher's prophetic posture of saving the people by any and all means within his power, is it not true that in a figurative — if not a real — sense that he must be considered to be in the [hell] fire insurance business? Has the glue hardened on the tenuous tie that binds him to the new discovery that one cannot do full justice to his calling when he is saddled with other demanding exactions?

It is possible that the parishioners within the church, by the lavish outpouring of pastoral extravagance, might themselves reap direct benefits. Perhaps the members of the churches should rejoice at the dissipation of such needed services performed far and wide, as they release the pastor to such missions of helpfulness. For such sharing, might not an unchurched, unbaptized throng graciously one day rise up and call them — the church members — blessed?

Would Marshall Shepard, rugged individualist and independent to the core as he was, have resisted, chafed over, resigned from the church if the congregation had not allowed him the freedom to do so many other things? It is a matter for rejoicing that the black church of his Philadelphia days never went so far as to present Shep with that kind of option. After all, his hometown is called the "City of Brotherly Love." Had the church forced a deliberate showdown, there might have been no Marshall Shepard as he was known. What a shame such a development would have been!

On February 26, 1967, a Service of Triumph was held in the First Baptist Church, Oxford, North Carolina. From the obituary distributed at that time, a paragraph reflects the man's renown:

> The psalmist says, "A man's gifts will cause him to stand before kings." This was manifested in the life of Reverend Shepard as he traveled throughout this country and world, exercising his gifts as a gospel preacher and public servant. His service to God and man and his intense desire to achieve the highest standard of excellence will be long remembered by the thousands whose lives were made richer and more meaningful because he passed this way.